Active Nonviolence

FOREWORD BY JOAN CHITTISTER, O.S.B.

ACTIVE NONVIOLENCE

A Way of Personal Peace

Gerard A. Vanderhaar

WIPF & STOCK · Eugene, Oregon

To Janice

my wife of twenty years
and inspiring companion
on the road to nonviolence.

Wipf and Stock Publishers
199 W 8th Ave, Suite 3
Eugene, OR 97401

Active Nonviolence
A Way of Personal Peace
By Vanderhaar, Gerard and Chittister, Joan, OSB
Copyright©1991 by Vanderhaar, Gerard
ISBN 13: 978-1-62564-273-8
Publication date 8/15/2013
Previously published by Twenty-Third Publications, 1991

FOREWORD

Camus wrote once: The saints of our times are those who refuse to be either its executioners or its victims.

And Augustine wrote: The sword with which we would destroy the other must pass first through our own hearts.

The concept of nonviolence, about which *Active Nonviolence: A Way of Personal Peace* is written, is a living acknowledgment of the truth of these insights. In the first place, the vow of nonviolence calls out the best in us of both courage and compassion. The popular image in a culture that puts plastic machine guns in the hands of seven year olds for Christmas presents is that nonviolence is a weakness. We work hard at bringing up children who are hard, not soft. We want a nation of impregnable steel in a world of penetrable boundaries. We want to heap up things far beyond what we need and stockpile weapons far beyond a usable number, even to the military mind, and have and hoard and control far beyond the conscionable. But it is restraint that takes strength. It is patience that takes strength. It is love that takes strength.

But retaliation, name-calling, hatred, and violence (even violent accumulation)—they are easy. And they are cowardly, too. They can all be done behind closed doors and without substantiation. They all deny respect to the other. They all give the lie to reverence. They all imply that force is the answer.

But force wasn't able to maintain slavery, or secure the British Empire, or exterminate the Jews. Force cannot today contain the anti-apartheid movement, nor is it making the globe safer or the people of the earth more peaceful. It is not a pretty picture, this display of power without compassion.

When I have really learned to suffer with the other—the poor, the voiceless, the marginated, the people without power—I'll begin to see a whole new world. I'll begin to see the violence around me and in me. I'll begin to see the need to refuse to cooperate with it. I'll begin to see what I never saw before. What middle-class American can imagine what it's like not to be able to drive to work in the morning? What middle-class American has ever been in a soup line? What middle-class American is on the run from destitution or from governments that make people "disappear" because they organize labor unions or teach liberation theology? What middle-class American can even really imagine that anyone can want the basics of life and not be able to have them? They can work themselves up, we say. They can get it the hard way, like the rest of us, we say. If people are willing to work, we say, they can always get a job even if it's only sweeping streets or digging ditches or washing dishes. But that truism was formulated, surely, in the era before street cleaning machines, and back hoes, and dishwashers. That cliche was the working person's national anthem only before the government chose to invest in destruction instead of in human development.

There is no doubt: it takes courage to face down a violent generation without becoming like them. It takes courage to stop violence by refusing to continue it. It takes courage to absorb the amount of punishment required to rob the brutal of the joy of their brutality and to turn the tide of this senselessness.

The little people who faced the dogs in Selma to gain their humanity, the tiny women who climb the fences of nuclear installations to pray for their dismantling, the little groups who sign petition after petition to stop planetary pollution, the little boats that obstruct the wanton killing of dolphins and whales, the myriad little people who refuse to be willing victims of an age more given to death than to life—these are seeds of a new human consciousness, a new global soul.

Indeed, compassion and courage—the commitment to be neither executioner nor victim—are of the essence of nonviolence.

Gerard Vanderhaar's book invites each of us to wrestle with the violence in our own lives, our own lifestyle, our own hearts. *Active Nonviolence* tells us that we can join the ranks of the compassionate and courageous by having violence end where my boundaries begin. This book describes the effect of violence on our own lives. It cautions us to look for violence where the violence that is poisoning the planet and its peoples lurks least noticed: within me, in the way I talk, in the way I treat myself, in the way I deal with the people nearest and dearest to me, in the way I go about my life, in the way even that I work for the goods of the gospel. This book shows me how to be gentle with myself and how to be gentle with others.

There is a rich literature of the theology, philosophy, and history of nonviolence, but there is little enough of the light of nonviolence being brought to the pace and parts of our own private lives. Vanderhaar's book begins to do that. It is a good gift in hard times, a gentle blessing. This book is manageable and understandable and profound in its implications.

Active Nonviolence beckons us all, whoever we are, however we live, to come into the kind light of peace-filled days in our own lives. For the sake of the rest of the world, let us all begin.

Joan D. Chittister, O.S.B.

Whatever is right, whatever is pure,
whatever is lovely, whatever is admirable—
if anything is excellent or praiseworthy—
think about such things.

Philippians 4:8

CONTENTS

Foreword by Joan D. Chittister, O.S.B.   *v*

PART ONE
PERSONAL NONVIOLENCE

Chapter 1 – Nonviolence in a Violent World	2
Chapter 2 – A Philosophy of Nonviolence	8
Chapter 3 – Life-Affirming Truth	15
Chapter 4 – Personal Best	19

PART TWO
NONVIOLENT SPEECH

Chapter 5 – A Nonviolent Dialect	24
Chapter 6 – A Manner of Speaking	30
Chapter 7 – Nonviolent Criticism	36

PART THREE
NONVIOLENCE TOWARD MYSELF

Chapter 8 – Personal Peace	42
Chapter 9 – Healthy Self-Love	49

PART FOUR
NONVIOLENT CONFLICT RESOLUTION

Chapter 10 – Nonviolent Winning	56
Chapter 11 – Cooperation and Trust	65

PART FIVE
NONVIOLENT RESPONSE TO ASSAULT

Chapter 12 – Personal Assault	76
Chapter 13 – Dynamics of a Nonviolent Response	83
Chapter 14 – It Can Work	90

PART SIX
NONVIOLENT PUBLIC RELATIONS

Chapter 15 – Courteous Assertion	96
Chapter 16 – Fringe Benefits	101

PART SEVEN
A NONVIOLENT LIFESTYLE

Chapter 17 – To Live Decently	107
Chapter 18 – Simpler Living	114
Chapter 19 – Money Problems	121

PART EIGHT
NONVIOLENT IMPATIENCE

Chapter 20 – Inward Discontent	127
Chapter 21 – Nonviolent Revenge	134
Chapter 22 – A Different Drumbeat	138
Notes	144
Bibliography	151

PART ONE

PERSONAL NONVIOLENCE

The kind of strong, active, effective nonviolence pioneered in our century by people like Mohandas Gandhi and Martin Luther King, Jr., and Dorothy Day can influence our personal lives very deeply. It can color what we say, what we do, how we think. We may not do great deeds, move mountains, or change the world, but the way we meet the multiple challenges that confront us every day can make a great difference in our lives, and in the lives of those around us. To live in this troublesome world in a spirit of nonviolence can bring out the very best in a person and place us squarely on the road to personal peace.

◦ 1 ◦

NONVIOLENCE IN A VIOLENT WORLD

Most of us aren't going to be famous—Presidents or Prime Ministers, celebrities or superstars. Our lot will be to slog through the trenches every day, stumbling over one or other unforeseen obstacle, trying to meet our responsibilities. We do some things nicely, others haphazardly. We make mistakes. Some people like us; others don't. We try to get by.

Presidents and Prime Ministers are in the spotlight, but they're human too. They also have to slog through the trenches. They have to deal with difficult people, make decisions that affect lives for better or worse, wade through oceans of trivia—like all the rest of us.

And we all have to do it in the climate of a violent and dangerous world. Muggings, drugs, hijackings are perennial possibilities. Racism, sexism, imperialism affect us sorely. And over everything the specter of nuclear war clouds the horizon.

Spiritual Need

In the midst of the murk there is a deep spiritual hunger abroad, the desire for something better, something more meaningful. Witness the televangelists' persistent appeal or the intense enthusiasm that greets charismatic musical groups. The traditional churches and synagogues satisfy that hunger for some, national or cultural ideologies do it for others. But for many who live in the more developed northern world, east and west, for whom day-to-day survival is not a pressing problem, the religious institutions and the prevailing ideologies have become so much a part of the status quo, the predictable humdrum of existence, that they no longer satisfy us as fully and no longer challenge us as they once did.

Everybody knows that television evangelists and rock musicians bring in millions of dollars, that they live quite comfortably, but that doesn't dampen their mass appeal, despite public foibles. That doesn't stop people from being loyal followers, and continuing to contribute to their coffers. That's because they strike a chord, fill a need, point to something arousing, something beyond the hum-drum, something different from the daily dreariness.

The adulation of Elvis Presley more than a decade after his death continues to amaze us, until we understand that Elvis, too, even now, meets a spiritual need. The poor country boy who made good beyond his and our wildest dreams, who sparked a sexual revolution and still seemed to be a country boy, continues to touch the lives of people who want more, who are not resigned to the tedium of a troubled world.

It is in that context of spiritual need in a time of turmoil that I find the theory and practice of nonviolence so appealing.

Social and Personal

When we think of the kind of nonviolence practiced by Gandhi, King, and Day, images of mass marches, demonstrations, and arrests come to mind. They were a significant part of the stirring civil rights movement that King led in this country in the 1950s and 1960s. They were also part of the impressive liberation of India in the first half of this century influenced by the incomparable Mahatma Gandhi, the Great-Souled one, from whom King drew much of his inspiration.

The nonviolence pioneered by Gandhi in India and King in the United States has been used successfully in labor union strikes, grape boycotts, civil rights movements, anti-war protests, women's liberation—grand actions for political freedom and social change.

Dorothy Day, another model of nonviolence, was an American heroine who developed the influential Catholic Worker movement. She always insisted she wanted to *change* social conditions, but change them nonviolently. "I had lost faith in revolution," she wrote. "I wanted to love my enemy, whether capitalist or communist."

We are now aware that nonviolence can be more than a tactic for social struggle. It can be a guide to our personal life, our everyday encounters with other people. It can even help us cope with stress, that lurking giant of whose malevolent presence we are increasingly aware and respectful.

Shortly before he was killed, Martin Luther King wrote in a provocative aside, "I plan to stand by nonviolence because I have found it to be a philosophy of life that regulates not only my dealings in the struggle for racial justice but also my dealings with people, (and) with my own self."[1]

We know much about King's nonviolence in the struggle for racial and economic justice, and how surprisingly successful it was. He showed us how nonviolence could change the racial scene, help black and white Americans look on each other with a new appreciation and a heightened sense of shared humanity. But in the decades since his death we are only beginning to comprehend how these same principles of nonviolence can transform our personal lives.

King said that nonviolence was a philosophy of life that regulated his *dealings with people*. His tragic assassination robbed us of his developing ideas about how this could work. It also deprived us of his intriguing insights on how he tried to be nonviolent *with himself*. That's an interesting suggestion: How we can be nonviolent toward ourselves in the same active, positive way that we move the social agenda forward.

A Transformation

I am convinced that nonviolence can extend deep into our lives and bring about a personal transformation analogous to the political transformation King started. He showed us how America could achieve greatness by becoming a truly nonviolent nation. We haven't gotten there yet—we haven't even come close. But personal challenges confront each of us right now. Challenges of violence and discord in our daily lives—we can do something about these. We don't have to wait for anything else to happen. We can put ourselves on the course of nonviolence starting right now.

In the bigger picture, because there's no such thing as a nation apart from its people, we can help our nation become more nonviolent by being more nonviolent ourselves. Nonviolence will not become national policy until it is first the personal policy of millions of us.

But whether or not we have any real hope for the big picture, the personal realm is where most of us have to confront opposition and handle stress. Most of us are not involved in grand civil rights crusades or taking to the streets to end apartheid in South Africa or war in Central America, but we all face potential violence in our families, antagonisms at work, disagreements and crime in our neighborhood. We are all burdened by obligations and pressures that sometimes make us want to go off and hide.

Every time we're faced with a conflict, we have an opportunity to practice nonviolence. I remember the first time I consciously tried out Martin Luther King's insight about forgiveness, an essential ingredient in nonviolence, and how pleased I was when it worked. King said that forgiveness is not a sentimental blurring of a past offense, but a conscious refusal to let what happened in the past stand in the way of a present relationship. King did not say forgiving means forgetting. We shouldn't forget, lest the same circumstances bring about the same offense. But we shouldn't let that stand in the way of doing something positive *now*.[2]

Right after reading that, my wife and I had a disagreement. Whatever it was about, we quickly turned it to some past pattern of behavior on the part of one of us. Then something clicked—an inspiration or grace. King's explanation of forgiveness came to mind. I remember thinking, let's not get diverted into the past this time; let's stay on the present issue. It didn't take much to come back to the present, and concentrate on what we were arguing about. We began discussing our difference and we were able to resolve it rather quickly. It was such a relief not to be bogged down in the insoluble, not to attack past behavior, not to nurse hurt feelings. Nonviolence on a personal scale became instantly practical for me!

Everyone can concentrate on being more nonviolent in all such encounters and attempt to integrate the dynamics of nonviolence into all our activities. It works. Maybe not always or not perfectly, but better than most other approaches I know about. As a bonus, in practicing nonviolence we put ourselves in touch with the best in the religious traditions of West and East—Gandhi was a Hindu—and with the most noble social movements of our century.

In *Habits of the Heart*, their perceptive scrutiny of contemporary American mores, Robert Bellah and his colleagues called for reconstituting our "social ecology." They envisioned a movement that would be the successor and the fulfillment of the Civil Rights era. It would transform our society away from fragmentation and individualism and involve a common effort to share our resources more equitably.[3]

The personal nonviolence considered in this book does what they say needs to be done. It turns us outward, away from a self-centered concentration on the pursuit of personal happiness. It helps us increase our sensitivity to the needs of others, reach out and improve things for *them*. In doing so, we find that things improve for ourselves as well.

Working to improve the conditions of society is an integral part of nonviolence. But it is only a part. Nonviolence includes helpful relationships with everyone with whom we come in contact, especially the nearest "thou" at hand.

Of course this is also the Christian ideal: to love our neighbor as ourselves. It is also the humane, decent, and courteous way to live. Nonviolence is not different from the Christian ideal, or from a humane way of living. It is a special way of approaching that ideal. It locates our humane instincts in a particular historical tradition, the one pioneered by Gandhi and King and Day and others in our century.

We know they believed strongly in the message of Jesus, in the Sermon on the Mount, in the power of suffering love, but they took these grand ideals and lived them in a new way. It is that new way which we will explore to see how we can be nonviolent in our personal lives.

◎ 2 ◎

A PHILOSOPHY OF NONVIOLENCE

To practice this kind of nonviolence concretely, it helps to understand the basic ideas that underlie it. In this book I rely primarily on Gandhi and King, because they coupled their nonviolent actions and movements with extensive writing on the theory of nonviolence. That theory, and their actions, can serve us very well today.

Their nonviolence was first of all an action, a *doing* something. The most common misunderstanding about nonviolence is that it is a *non*-doing, a passivity, a refusal to be violent. It is an easy confusion to make, because the word itself is negative: *not* being violent. Many times people who want to avoid trouble, who sidestep confrontation, are said to be nonviolent. Sometimes they are, in the sense of Gandhi and King and Day. At other times they may simply be evasive. The nonviolence we are describing is not evasive. It is anything but negative. It does include the element of refusing to hurt others, the refusal that Gandhi called *ahimsa*, non-harm, which is the rock-bottom of nonviolence. But it is much more; it is vigorous, positive, and assertive *activity*.

A nonviolent person *does* things—speaks, walks, gesticulates, intervenes—and is constantly active in mind and emotions, trying to figure out what is happening and looking for effective ways of persuasion. Thinking about them ahead of time and creating a nonviolent attitude internally is essential preparation for our outward acts.

Nonviolent action takes courage. Gandhi was so insistent on this that he said if ever it came to a choice between violence or cowardice, we should choose violence. It is easier to sit back and let unpleasant things happen when we don't have the heart to try to correct them. But that laissez-faire attitude is a counterfeit nonviolence. King called it "stagnant passivity." True nonviolence takes inner energy, desire, and a willingness to risk.

Nonviolent action may be only a touch, a look, a calm word, but it always reaches out to help. The best definition I know of genuine nonviolence is *positive action for true human good, using only means that help and do not harm*. It is not haphazard, a restless expenditure of energy, but action along a definite helping line. It is based on a definite set of beliefs about people and about the cosmos.

People

All of us act the way we do because we believe the way we do. In nonviolence we believe something important first about individual people—that they are basically good. No matter how deplorably they act at times, we are convinced that people are fundamentally worthy of respect. This is the underlying meaning of the affirmation that life is sacred, that everyone is a daughter or son of God, that we are temples of the Holy Spirit. Some Eastern religions express this belief as the God within, others as the universality of the Buddha nature. They mean that everyone has the potentiality to reach spiritual heights, to obtain enlightenment, to be saved. There is hope for every person under the sun.

One major belief on which nonviolence is based is the fundamental dignity of all human beings. "Violence" comes from the

Latin *violare*, which means to injure or dishonor. Nonviolence is first of all the *refusal* to injure or dishonor another, physically or otherwise. We try to avoid hurting others, because everyone is valuable, and worthy of respect. Even when we're attacked or treated unjustly, we acknowledge the radical goodness of our opponents and refrain from striking back, from hurting in return. Jesus proposed a fundamental consequence of this belief when he said to forgive—again and again. How often, as many as seven times? "I do not say to you seven times, but seventy times seven" (Matt. 18:22). He wasn't being literal, meaning to forgive 490 times and that's enough. He was being symbolic, using the number for perfection, seven, with the number for a multitude, ten. Seven squared times ten is another way of putting seventy times seven. Jesus meant forgive again and again.

Gandhi once said, "Forgiveness is the ornament of the brave." Forgive, rather than lashing out to hurt. Forgive, rather than punishing. Forgive, because everyone is still capable of decency even after doing something wrong. But forgive the way King described it, not letting past offenses block the building of a present relationship. Forgive, but don't forget. Look out for trouble. The same set of circumstances can produce the same results again. Don't forget, so that you can see it coming the next time and ward it off. But forgive, let the affront pass, and be ready to start over again, because everyone can do better.

That there's hope for everyone under the sun is a very practical belief, derived from our experience and contributing to it. We know it works. Most of the time when we treat people as basically good they respond positively. Sometimes they don't. Sometimes they take advantage of our forgiveness and interpret it as weakness. We should not naively think people always act in the best way—sometimes they are morally ugly—but our conviction is that when they do mistreat us we still have a better way of responding than to be violent in return.

After being informed that her little girl was bitten by another child, one young mother was heard to tell her, "Did you bite her back?" Countless fathers have given advice in the same vein to their young sons about the "manly" way to respond to a playground punch. Too many people think that counterviolence is the only way to defend ourselves. But this cycle is self-defeating. As King pointed out, "Someone must have sense enough and morality enough to cut off the chain of hate. This can only be done by projecting the ethic of love to the center of our lives."[1]

"You have heard that it was said, 'Love your neighbor and hate your enemy.' But I tell you: Love your enemies" (Matt. 5:43-44). Jesus' formula of enemy love doesn't mean that we have to like those who harm us. Love, according to Aquinas, is an act of the will, not of the emotions. Love is the desire for the good of another, not necessarily *feeling* good about the other.

Jesus didn't say we would not have "enemies," those who would injure us in some way, or that we shouldn't have any, or that we should pretend we don't have any. But he did teach us a better way of dealing with them than punishing them, a better way than getting even by retaliating in some way.

We all have some enemies, even though we may be reluctant to call them that. Most of the enemies I encounter in everyday life would better be called "difficult people." I don't particularly like them because they act in an irritating way. They may not be assaulting me or robbing me or plotting to poison me, but they are hard to get along with, because what they do is obnoxious or just wrong.

We all have what the Swiss psychoanalyst Carl Jung called a "shadow," or dark side that makes us capable of doing unpleasant things. We can hurt others by a quick retort, playing one-upmanship, putting someone down so in order to feel superior, maneuvering our way into a favorable position at someone else's expense. We can acknowledge this in ourselves at the same time as we recognize it in others. The most effective way of responding to it is not in kind, not continuing the cycle, but instead, with patient engagement, reaching out to help rather than to hurt. Violence ends where love begins, as the Pax Christi slogan has it.

Cooperation

The second major belief on which nonviolence is based concerns the preferred way of conducting human interactions: We need others if we want to be whole ourselves. Something about us makes us reach out, share, try to connect with others. The world's great religious leaders all recognized that built-in tendency. They taught that salvation cannot be found for oneself alone, ignoring others. In the words of Vatican II, "It has pleased God to make human beings holy and save them not merely as individuals without any mutual bonds, but by making them into a single people."[2] A contemporary Buddhist put it another way: "Quality living is not done in isolation. It can only occur through deep personal relations in shared experience and community."[3]

Interchange with others is more helpful than it is difficult. The second basic belief underlying nonviolence suggests that the best form of interaction is cooperation, working together in a spirit of sharing. Charles Darwin's "survival of the fittest" theory notwithstanding, the philosophy of nonviolence declares that the human race has survived because of cooperation, not competition. Gandhi thought cooperation so important that he called it "a law of our species."[4]

This belief is reinforced pragmatically every time we see that cooperation improves the quality of our life. When we contribute something to others, it enhances our feeling of well-being. And, when we relax and let others into our life, we benefit tangibly when they do something that helps us.

Anyone associated with institutions these days hears a great deal about "management by objectives," "flow charts," "immediate supervisors." The philosophy of nonviolence does not include top-down managerial theory, no matter how neatly the operating manuals and long-range plans lay it out, no matter what its claims for efficiency. Nonviolence is based on the conviction that, because cooperation is a law of our species, people do their best work when they're encouraged and assisted, not when they're commanded or intimidated.

In a small Catholic college, the five-person department of which I'm a member has long had as its operational guide: "Hire good people and turn them loose." We believe in paying much attention to the ability of those who join us; then we try to give full latitude to their talents and interests, all of us encouraging and supporting each other. The only reason there is a chairperson is because college procedures call for it, and someone has to be the funnel through whom decisions go. But we try to take those decisions jointly. And we make sure the chair rotates among us every three years. The department, in a word, is trying to practice the basic principles of nonviolence: affirming the fundamental dignity of all and working together for the best interests of all—our students, our colleagues, and ourselves.

The Cosmos
The third basic belief that undergirds nonviolence is that not only individual people, but the universe itself is, on balance, good. Despite tornadoes, floods, forest fires, volcanoes, wild animals, poison plants, earthquakes, and a tenuous ozone layer, we believe that the whole thing tilts—ever so slightly, perhaps, but discernibly—toward good. God looked at creation, and "saw that it was good" (Gen. 1:25). Following God's lead, we view creation as cosmos rather than chaos, believing it is essentially harmonious, despite the frequency of its accidents.

Our intuition is that the randomness, the vastness, and the complexity of the universe in some as yet unfathomed way work for wholeness. We believe our environment is more conducive to growth than to suffering. That's what King meant when he said that the moral arc of the universe is long, but it bends toward justice. When we pursue that justice nonviolently, whether in the streets or right at home, we have what he called "cosmic companionship."

The Longer View
Nonviolence does not always appear to be a rational approach to a problem. In the short term, violence may appear more effective. Consider the single mother in California who, finding her neighborhood growing increasingly dangerous, bought a gun. "I decided that I would defend myself and my son, even if it meant killing another person," she said.[5] But, stepping back, and taking a longer view, realizing that violence breeds violence, realizing also that the cycle can be broken—it must be broken for our neigh-

borhood, not to mention our world, to survive—we know beyond our momentary gut feeling that nonviolence is a compelling call.

Some people dismiss as naive romanticism or futile moralizing such advice as, "Live in harmony with one another; be sympathetic, love as brothers (and sisters), be compassionate and humble. Do not repay evil with evil or insult with insult, but with blessing, because to this you were called" (I Pet. 3:8-9). When we're sensitive to nonviolence, we don't consider these words romantic or moralizing. We see it rather as a summary of nonviolent conduct, presented in the context of a "calling." It's the way things are meant to be.

◉ 3 ◉

LIFE-AFFIRMING TRUTH

Thomas Merton suggested that anyone who even dimly feels a need for truth "should seek it by way of nonviolence, since there really is no other way. They may not fully succeed. Their success may in fact be very slight. But for a small measure of good will they will at least *begin* to attain the truth."[1] In linking truth with nonviolence Merton was following Gandhi, whose word for active, disciplined nonviolence was *satyagraha*, translated as "truth force," or insistence on truth. The Sanskrit word *sat*, truth, at root means "is", or "being." It implies that the most fundamental truth is existence itself. Gandhi believed that truth is whatever is life-affirming, whatever contributes to a fuller human existence.

This important insight cuts through a philosophical thicket. When Pilate asked Jesus, "What is truth?" (John 18:38), he was posing a question that philosophers have considered for millennia, with varying results. But Pilate wasn't being philosophical. He was just casting a wistful glance in the direction Jesus had pointed: "Everyone on the side of truth listens to me" (John 18:37), before making the messy decision of a mediocre bureaucrat muddling through.

Gandhi's criterion for whether an action is true or false, good or bad, is whether or not it is *conducive to human well-being*.[2] His insight about the meaning of truth coincides with Vatican II's stress on "the duty to build a better world," what it called "the birth of a new humanism."[3] When we engage in this demanding work, we are pointed in the direction of truth.

Truth and Harm

But, Gandhi rightly insisted, we cannot always know what is true, what is conducive to human well-being in certain circumstances. None of us has a monopoly on truth. He saw this as another reason for *ahimsa*. We don't have the right to punish somebody for violating truth because we may be seeing only a partial aspect of it. They may have another aspect.

What we're trying to do in nonviolence is to create an atmosphere to clarify the truth. So we need to know whatever there is of it in the opponent's position as well as our own, whether our opponent at the moment is our spouse, a child at home, a colleague, a supervisor at work, an intrusive salesman, a police officer writing a ticket, our city council representative, or the President of the United States.

In our Mertonian search for truth there's no way we're going to avoid causing some harm. Nonviolence does not insist on perfection. Although Gandhi taught that we should strive for *ahimsa*, he recognized that we are all caught up in some degree in *himsa*. We cannot go for long without consciously or unconsciously committing some outward hurt in our human encounters.[4]

What we can do is become increasingly sensitive to the damage we inflict on others, the emotional hurt, the unintended slight, and try to lower its level or reverse its direction. We won't eliminate it altogether, but we will cut it back as our awareness becomes more acute.

Accepting Hurt

Nonviolence is a way of looking at the world, at the people around us, and saying no to the distress and ugliness, the exploitation and violence, but also saying yes to all which can heal the distress, transform the ugliness and remove the exploitation. That doesn't just mean *saying* no to the violence, but by *doing* something to end it. Seek the truth by acting for the truth.

Our active grappling with trouble will often lead us to a point where we can get hurt. At those critical times the spirit of nonviolence is to accept suffering rather than inflict it. We have to be prepared to shoulder the sacrifice, accept the hurt ourselves, rather than imposing it on our opponent.

Our willingness to accept abuse without retaliation can make the attacker stop. One married couple I know sometimes ends an argument in this way. The wife, instead of arguing back, has been known to look at him squarely, cringe exaggeratedly, and say, "Hit me again." They stop, he laughs, they make up.

In other situations the turnaround may not be as quick, or may not happen at all. After a visit to Nicaragua I wrote some Letters to the Editor and gave several talks on why it was misleading to label Nicaragua a Communist country. Anonymous letters began arriving at home. I was denounced publicly and repeatedly for being at best a dupe, if not an actual participant in the "Communist conspiracy." My inclination was to fight back, attack the attackers publicly and in print, show them up for being uninformed and prejudiced. But I decided, in the spirit of nonviolence, to accept whatever humiliation they wanted to dish out rather than engaging in personal counter-attacks. And when I did respond I tried to keep my remarks focused on the issues, and not demean the persons. I hoped to have better success in having my ideas accepted if I did not engage in personal acrimony.

But accepting public criticism, stinging as it is, is much easier than enduring fire hoses and police dogs, as King's people did in the Civil Rights era, or the blows of police clubs and British bullets, as Gandhi's people did in freeing India. King reminded us of the way Gandhi had put it:

> Rivers of blood may have to flow before we gain our freedom, but it must be our blood... Suffering is infinitely more powerful than the law of the jungle for convert-

ing the opponent and opening ears which are otherwise shut to the voice of reason.[5]

When I think of rivers of blood, a little public or private criticism is paltry by comparison. We free ourselves from the manipulative attempts of others to the extent that we are willing to suffer, maybe a little but sometimes more, instead of inflicting harm on them and compounding the problem. To Christians it is called the theology of the cross.

Pursuit of Happiness

The truth of nonviolence goes against the conventional microwisdom of accumulating for ourselves. A life based on maximizing one's self-interest is in the long run self-defeating. When we seriously and single-mindedly pursue our own happiness, when we always try to arrange circumstances to enhance our own personal fulfillment, pleasure, or joy, we find that happiness eludes us.

Nonviolence transmutes the cultural version of the pursuit of happiness from self-serving to self-giving. It involves openness, responsiveness, and a certain flowing with events rather than always trying to put one's stamp on them.

Nonviolence is in harmony with the deeper truth, the paradox that in giving we receive, in loving we are loved, in dying we rise to a new life.

◉ 4 ◉

PERSONAL BEST

Jesus pointed out that coming to appreciate the dynamic of the cross in our lives is a wonderfully liberating experience. "If anyone would come after me," he said, that person must "take up (the) cross daily and follow me" (Luke 9:23). If you do that, "if you hold to my teaching, you are really my disciples. Then you will know the truth, and the truth will set you free" (John 8:32).

Martin Luther King, Jr. knew that setting out on the road of nonviolence would involve the cross. But it would also help people to be free and to become better than they were. He said:

> Another of the major strengths of the nonviolent weapon is its strange power to transform and transmute the individuals who subordinate themselves to its disciplines, investing them with a cause that is larger than themselves. They become, for the first time, somebody, and they have, for the first time, the courage to be free.[1]

Many people hesitate to take that step in the direction of the cross, make the change toward nonviolence, start to become really free, and become better persons. They allow themselves to be sidetracked by the values and titillation of television, or lured by the seduction of shopping malls. They succumb to the struggle for survival, at whatever level they are resigned to, and give up the struggle for a nobler, richer, and nonviolent life.

Lights of the World

Others continue to search through the transience and turmoil of life for the elusive qualities that are part of personal growth. For them the spark remains. The ideal of personal best has a strong appeal. At first we might feel uneasy with the phrase, "personal best." It sounds too much like "Be all you can be (in the Army)." It evokes images of football crowds waving outsized gloves and shouting, "We're number one." What ever happened to humility?

Jesus didn't use the words "personal best." But he did say, "You are the light of the world" (Matt. 5:14), and "Let your light shine." But don't let it shine for yourself. Don't pin ribbons on your chest so everybody can see how great you are. Don't try to win through intimidation or build the biggest house on the block. Rather, Jesus said, let your light shine so that people may see your good deeds and praise your God in heaven (Matt. 5:16). Let it shine, but let it shine to benefit others, not just yourself. Let it shine for the Cause.

An Experiment

All self-help books have two themes in common: that we can change for the better and that to do so we have to learn certain techniques. The same is true for nonviolence. It can improve our living, and for that to happen we have to master certain techniques.

We're sure of some of these techniques, such as the development of communication skills, so that we can share our aspect of the truth and encourage others to share theirs with us. We want to draw out the truth in others rather than suppress them for the non-truth they may be communicating.

But we're not sure of *everything* nonviolence requires. We're still in the exploratory stages. Mohandas Gandhi had his way of living nonviolently in India, with his community ashrams, his times of solitude and spinning, his family life. Dorothy Day did it differently in the Catholic Worker house in New York City, ministering to the down and out, living an intense intellectual and spiritual life in the midst of constant activity. Martin Luther King, Jr., lived nonviolently in a middle-class setting. Many Latin American Christians in base communities are models of nonviolence in a culture of deprivation and exploitation. We look to all of them for guidance.

Gandhi called his nonviolence an "experiment in truth." When we decide to make our lives as nonviolent as possible, we too will engage in much experimentation. At such times we may be criticized for our inconsistency, or be told that the track we're on is not the right track.

We listen to the criticism, size it up, then either move with it if it feels right or gently put it aside because it doesn't seem right for us, remembering that those who offer it are experimenting with life just as we are.

I like the way peace activist and theologian Jim Douglass has described the experiment in nonviolence:

> We experience nonviolent change as a mystery of grace, like watching a bird take to the air. The illusion of violence is that we can effect whatever change we want in the world by forcing someone else to accept it. The mystery of nonviolent change is the discovery that patient experiments in truthful action have a power to change relationships in the world beyond anything we imagined. The effect of an experiment in nonviolence is like the flight of a bird released from our hands. Nonviolence has a power of grace to soar beyond our own vision and control.[2]

An Invitation

This book is not written to persuade the reader to be nonviolent. It is for those who already feel a kinship with Gandhi, Day,

King, and others like them, who see possibilities for a more peaceful world, and who want to fine-tune their lives in keeping with this developing tradition. And it is not meant to convey a sense of moral superiority, or to judge anyone who acts differently from ways described here. The book is an invitation to explore nonviolence in daily life, to recognize the many ways we can hurt others, to reduce those ways of being violent, substituting positive nonviolent approaches instead.

This is also not a handbook for social activism. It is an invitation to believe that a nonviolent attitude and nonviolent actions, however we work them out in our own experiments with truth, are the best available options for personal as well as political living in this complex, often cruel, and certainly demanding existence we call life.

PART TWO

NONVIOLENT SPEECH

In trying to be more nonviolent in our personal lives, a good place to start is with our speech. It is not too difficult to become more careful of what we say and how we say it. When we speak with an eye to nonviolence, we are more sensitive to the fact that some things we say can communicate an atmospere of disrespect, even of harm. We also grow more conscious of the nonviolent spirit our words can convey.

◎ 5 ◎

A NONVIOLENT DIALECT

Something significant is at stake whenever we talk. Jesus said we would "have to give account on the day of judgment for every careless word" we speak (Matt. 12:36). That's a strong warning. Whenever we speak, no matter how relaxed we feel, how casual the context, we are responsible for what we say.

Speaking is what philosophers call a person's *mode of being*. Language essentially is the opening of oneself to another. Dutch theologian Edward Schillebeeckx called it "a revelation."[1] When we speak, we speak about something, perhaps as commonplace as the weather or as controversial as international politics. But in the act of speaking we also communicate something else, something about ourselves. What's at stake when we speak is our inner life, what or who we really are.

The Heart Speaks

That's what Jesus was referring to when he said that it's not what goes into the mouth that defiles a person, but what comes out of it, because "the things that come out of the mouth come from the heart" (Matt. 15:18). Something inside us is expressed by our words. "Out of the overflow of the heart the mouth speaks" (Matt. 12:34). Not only the words we choose, but also our manner of speaking—calm or excited, peremptory or tentative—reveals what we feel, who we are. We speak from what we are.

This self-revelation occurs unless, of course, we're acting, pretending to be something we're not. Theatrical professionals have to undergo training to do this. Their job demands that they speak the lines, no matter what they're feeling within themselves. It's hard to do, consistently. By hard work they can learn at least how to *appear* to be feeling what their words are saying. And the better actors and actresses learn actually to conjure up the feelings to match the words, to cry real tears, to laugh on cue.

Politicians sometimes try to do this, not always with the same skill. So do salespeople, and television personalities. They often appear to be insincere, even hypocritical (which comes from a Greek word that meant playing a part on a stage). And indeed they are insincere, as is everyone who speaks something other than what's really in the heart.

In actors and actresses we expect insincerity, because it's their job. In politicians we're coming to accept it, because it seems to be an inevitable accompaniment to holding public office. They have to say what they imagine large numbers of people want to hear, whether or not what they say actually reflects what they're really thinking at the time.

But to speak something different from what we are is hard to do convincingly, because it goes against our nature. That's why lie detectors work. They measure changes in body temperature and pulse rate, signs of the tension that usually accompanies saying something other than what we really feel.

It's also why so many theatrical people have problems with emotional soundness. Their profession calls for them constantly to be putting on a different face, pretending to be something they're not. And even when they're being true to themselves, speaking authentically, we are not sure how to take them, because we know that the very appearance of authenticity can also be an act.

But normally we assume that when someone speaks we can

learn something about the *person* as well as about the subject being expressed. From the other side of that coin, as we strive to be more nonviolent, we want to communicate a nonviolent spirit in our speech. We certainly want to avoid directly abusing others, shouting at them angrily, humiliating them, lying about them. These are obvious forms of violent speech. When we find ourselves inflicting emotional harm with our words, we want to work on changing our mode of speech.

A New Dialect

But there are other, more subtle ways of harming others, some of them indirect, even unintentional. Besides violent speech, there is the speech of violence. That happens when we use words that convey a climate of violence, many of which are military jargon, even though we don't intend to commit the violence implied in the words.

We hear people say, "Fire away," when they're ready to be questioned. And if they don't answer the questions correctly, they get "blown away," or "shot down." Advertisers "target" a certain audience. An announcer gives "a blow by blow description." An editor "kills the story."

These are metaphors, colorful expressions, and can be used rhetorically to good advantage. But they are drawn from the world of violence, actions that hurt people and destroy property. They are part of the speech of violence. A nonviolent person eventually has to learn what is almost another language. It's not entirely new, but the kind of variation on common usage that's called a dialect. It tries to avoid words that convey images of violence, and instead uses phrases that are either neutral or positively supportive. We want to mitigate the aura of violence, not reinforce it.

Instead of telling a questioner to "fire away," the nonviolent dialect would suggest, "What would you like to know?" Rather than "kill the story," we use a more neutral phrasing, like "Delete it," or "Don't print it." We avoid descriptions like "They booby-trapped my project," preferring instead a calmer statement such as "I ran into serious opposition."

Most of what are commonly called "four letter words" communicate an atmosphere of abuse. Some imply violating another person sexually. Others refer crudely to bodily functions in a way that offends sensitivities. Still others are drawn from the realm of religion but used in a way that trivializes. The nonviolent dialect does not include words that offend in this way.

But this manner of speech, this new dialect is not necessarily bland or colorless. Instead of "We've got to get it in our sights" we could say, "Let's keep our eyes on the prize." An expression "Kill two birds with one stone" can become "Feed two birds with one crust."

When we say something that evokes a violence-related image because we didn't think of an alternative expression, or we just slipped up out of an old habit, at least we can show we're aware of it, and laugh. "Let's line up the troops and get going. Oh! I forgot. I'm trying to be nonviolent. What I meant was, Let's call in our friends and have a dialogue."

The starting point in developing a nonviolent dialect is becoming more aware of the connotations and implications of what we're saying.

A Practice of Prejudice

Conscious of *ahimsa*, we become increasingly sensitive to language that is sexist, racist, or ethnically disparaging. These usages have contributed to a tradition of discrimination that has tolerated and often encouraged violence against those considered weaker, or secondary, in society.

When it was assumed that women were inferior to men, it seemed natural to use masculine words referring to both genders: "A person should watch what he says." "Who's going to man the booth this afternoon?" "We believe in brotherhood and fellowship." That kind of practice was acceptable, sophomores were told, because, after all, "man" embraces "woman."

Since in the not too distant past masculine-dominated grammar was taught as orthodox, anyone brought up in those times has to take care to adjust the syntax. It takes practice to develop a habit of using generic rather than gender-specific terms. Once the doorbell rang and I went to the front door and asked, "Who is it?" A female voice replied, "Mailperson." Another time the voice identified herself with the term that is becoming more standard, "mail carrier."

When certain professions employed only males, "policeman" or "fireman" were accurate terms. Now, instead, a nonviolent dialect uses "police officer," or "fire fighter." Or "stunt specialist" or "spokesperson" (although some prefer to be specific and say "spokeswoman" if it is, or "chairwoman.") The converse is also true, as men have taken up some traditionally female work. So we say "flight attendant" instead of "stewardess," and "homemaker" instead of "housewife." Or if the situation is right we could say "househusband."

We no longer talk about a "male nurse," or a "lady doctor." "Fellowship" becomes "companionship" or "sharing." And "sister student" is more accurate than "fellow student" if we're referring to a female. Fifteen years after it began admitting women, Dartmouth College changed the name of its school song from "Men of Dartmouth" to "Alma Mater."

Racist language is as offensive as sexist language. New York Yankees owner George Steinbrenner was rightly taken to task when he said of a black employee, "I've got a good boy up there in the accounting office." A nonviolent dialect avoids such slur words. It also avoids usages that imply inferiority because of color. Bad guys don't always wear the black hats. A black sheep may be strikingly beautiful. And a black mark on someone's record can be made with a black felt-tip pen and be an annotation of excellence.

A nonviolent person will also be careful about ethnic overtones. We won't want to disparage a particular group of people by implying unfavorable characteristics, even when our intent is only to tell a joke. "How many southerners does it take to change a light bulb? Four: one to screw in a new bulb, and three others to sit around and talk about how good the old one was." That might be appropriate when told about oneself, or when members of the ethnic group present have enough self-possession to be able to laugh at themselves. But unless we're sure of the situation, it's best to avoid ethnic jokes.

Right Speech

In the Buddhist tradition a person setting out on the road to spiritual improvement is encouraged early on to work on speech: what to say and how to say it. On the Buddha's Eightfold Path to enlightenment "right speech" comes third, directly after "right views" and "right aspirations." After a novice has right views—knows the direction in which to go—and then decides to embark on it—right aspirations—the Buddha taught that the first practical step to take is to begin sharpening an awareness of the potential of language. Only when we know the full implications of our words can we begin to control what we're saying. That awareness and control is what the Buddha meant by "right speech."

That is what we seek in a nonviolent dialect—awareness first, and then the control that comes from developing and using alternative phrases. As we improve our speech in the direction of nonviolence, we will at the same time be improving our heart in the same direction. In developing a nonviolent dialect, we will also be developing a nonviolent heart.

◎ 6 ◎

A MANNER OF SPEAKING

Most people with whom we converse won't be skilled in a nonviolent dialect. Some will be aggressive, asserting their own egos and putting others down. Others will talk much more than they listen. Some will tend to withdraw, cringe, and not take part in the conversation.

A good thing about nonviolence is that it is unilateral; we can start it ourselves and not imitate other modes of speech. The point is to strive to be consistently nonviolent in the way we express ourselves. That means being quietly confident with the big talkers, sympathetic with the incessant talkers, gentle and nurturing with the fearful talkers.

Liberating Language

With all kinds of talkers it means being sensitive to the nuances of our words. Instead of characterizing someone as "stubborn," we might say that the person is "consistent," or "holds fast to an idea." That gets the same point across, but in a positively slanted way. Rather than "scatterbrained," a person might be called "enthusiastic" or "lively." Instead of disparaging someone by saying "I guess you couldn't handle it," we might observe, "That was quite a challenge." The point of this sensitive speech is to aim for a "we're in this together" atmosphere. We want to communicate an attitude of being helpful to others, reinforcing and encouraging their good instincts. A nonviolent dialect liberates rather than suppresses, supports rather than withdraws.

One effective way to give support to a conversation partner is to respond directly to what has been said, rather than to commence on our own train of thought.

Before I learned how to listen, I would frequently find myself interrupting, because what the other was saying would jog something in me, and I would blurt it out. A friend said, "Last week my motor scooter got stolen." I would interrupt, "Last year our car was stolen." Someone I hadn't seen for a while told me, "I just had my appendix out." I was quick to jump in, "Oh, I had cataract surgery."

When I'm interrupted as I'm trying to articulate an idea, I feel left hanging, awkward. In the same way, it is abrasive to others when I interrupt them, cutting in and preventing the development of their thought. When I jump in like that I may be slighting the other person, even being a bit rude. My enthusiasm may be attractive, but it doesn't justify the slight squelch I've just administered.

When I talk, I like it if others show they understand me, or at least have heard me. I can help others to that same comfortable feeling by affirming that I have heard and appreciate what they have said. It might just be by a nod of agreement, or perhaps a question that encourages the other to continue. "We went to Europe last summer." "Great. It must have been a wonderful experience. What countries did you visit?"

An appropriate response could be only a few reinforcing words, such as, "That must have been an interesting trip." It can even take the form of simply repeating the last words in a sentence, to show I'm listening. "When we got to Rome, I was surprised to see all those old ruins." I might just say,"...old ruins," which will encourage the person to continue.[1]

Another way to support a conversation partner is to respond when we are complimented. "You did a great job," someone tells me. I may feel like replying, "Oh, I really didn't. I thought it was pretty average." The complimenter could take my response as disagreeing with his or her judgment, or that I am rebuffing a gesture of good will. A nonviolent dialect contains a collection of appreciative reactions, involving a quick smile and a variation of "Thank you, I'm glad you liked it."

Active Listening

Because it's purpose is to liberate, silence is an important ingredient in a nonviolent dialect. By our timely quiet we can free another to talk, to express feelings, to share ideas. Liberating silence is not just an impatient pause, a polite restraint to give the other a turn until I can jump in again, it's a silence that involves my concentrated attention to what the other is saying— *active listening*.

I used to love to give advice, interjecting my solution to someone else's problem. I thought I had some pretty good ideas and wanted to share them. Someone would say, "I've been having a lot of trouble with my car lately. The mechanic at the gas station can't seem to fix it." I would respond, "I know this wonderful little shop where they specialize in your make of car. You should take it there." I couldn't understand why, when I started to give my solution, the other person would stop talking, sometimes start to look blank—and then not follow my advice. It took me a long time to learn to go slow with my suggestions. It finally dawned on me that I only had part of the truth, if that much. I came to realize that only after someone had fully expressed the trouble—and not always then—was there possible room for my suggestions.

Now I believe it's usually better to sympathize than to advise. It's better to say, "I'm sorry. You must feel pretty bad about not being able to get your car fixed." Then, if I get a signal that the person really wants my suggestions, I can offer them.

A nonviolent dialect includes space, keeping quiet, turning off my own words. I have to tell myself to be still and listen. Long-time friends who are used to each other's conversational ways might take interruptive patterns for granted. But even here, developing a nonviolent dialect with its active listening component can strengthen the friendship and make talking together even more rewarding.

Keep quiet for a while and let the other tell about the stolen motor scooter, or the appendectomy, or the car that kept breaking down. My turn will come. And if it doesn't, I have at least contributed to the other's sense of well-being by fulfilling the role of a good listener.

"I Propose"

There are times when we need to assert our ideas, to put forward our suggestions about what ought to be done when others are genuinely looking for advice. Even here a nonviolent dialect is helpful. One rainy Sunday my wife and I and several Belgian friends had taken the train from Antwerp to Brussels to take part in a giant peace rally. We emerged from the train station not being sure where to go to join the march. A young man in our group, taking the initiative, said, "I propose we go this way." I liked his way of putting it. He proposed, he didn't pressure. I felt relieved by his gentle suggestion, reassured by his familiarity with the scene. So did the others. We went where he proposed, and it turned out to be the right direction.

When we say, "Let's do it this way," or "What we ought to do is..." we put our personal force into the suggestion. The others have to deal not just with my idea, but with my ego, not just with *what* I'm saying, but with what *I'm* saying. They may feel uncomfortable with the pressure. But when I *propose* something, or suggest something, or use some other gentle way of putting forward my idea, it's offered in a form that can be accepted or not. "Propose" presents a softer image. People seem not to be as pushed by it, and usually respond positively when they understand that I'm offering a suggestion, not investing my ego in a demand. If they like the idea, fine. If they don't, then let's get together and figure out something better.

The Right Tone

Courtesy and considerateness are hallmarks of a nonviolent dialect. Sometimes the rub is not so much what we way, but how we say it.

A nonviolent person, tuned in to the hearing needs of others, will be careful to speak loudly enough to be heard clearly, but not so loud as to be jarring. A nonviolent dialect is spoken at a moderate level, neither shouting nor whispering—unless, of course, we're talking to someone who's hard of hearing.

Jumpy or excited speech patterns have a place at jumpy or excited times. In normal conversations they can be upsetting. They are especially upsetting when we talk with people for whom English is a second language. Our normal speed will probably be too fast for them. With a nonviolent dialect we will speak more slowly, more distinctly, enunciating in a way that would otherwise seem forced and artificial, but now is designed to be sensitive to the language of others.

Our voices are like musical instruments, embodying our emotions. Our vocal tones can be gentle and soothing, or sharp and demanding. If our sound is abrasive, no matter how well-intentioned we are, our words strike out stridently and cause sensitive people to draw back. But if our words are smooth and supportive, others will tend to feel more calm. A level, well modulated, conversational voice does not distract by communicating unpleasant sounds.

A simple request for information, "What time will you get home today?" can be spoken imperiously, pressing for an answer. "Where are you going?" with an emphasis on "going" and a downturn of voice communicates a demand. Asked with a soft swing in the middle ending in a slightly elevated tone, the same question will be seen as a desire for friendly sharing. What is sometimes called the Irish lilt, words delivered lightly, with an upswing and a hint of smile, suggests gentleness rather than force, pleasure rather than pressure.

As with all aspects of a new dialect, the right tone doesn't come automatically. It's a skill that has to be learned. A tape recorder can help. Listening to the way we speak can offer clues to problems we have with speed, volume, and inflection, which may need work. A wife can help a husband, a friend a friend. Our trusted partner can also remind us when we've gotten off the track in public.

Although the nonviolent dialect's starting point is *ahimsa*, it also includes encouragement and affirmation, the correlatives of non-harm. It helps us communicate not only clearly, but supportively. This kind of communication is part of the *action* of nonviolence.

7

NONVIOLENT CRITICISM

Careless, spontaneous, insensitive criticism almost always hurts. That's why Dale Carnegie, the celebrated instructor of effective interpersonal communication, used to say that the most important idea in dealing with others is "Don't criticize." Nobody likes to be told that what they're doing is wrong, that they have made a mistake. But in our desire to feel superior we often experience the inclination to put others down, to gain our altitude at the expense of their descent.

Whenever we feel like criticizing, whether people who are absent or someone present, a caution light should automatically go on. "Danger. Proceed carefully, if at all." We need to do a quick check of our motives. Are we about to criticize because we're irked? "Turn that radio down. It's driving me crazy!" Perhaps we want to make them feel uncomfortable. "You shouldn't have bought that jacket. It looks terrible on you." Do we have a better way of doing something and would like to see them do it our way? "You'd save a lot of time if you learned to use a word processor instead of that old typewriter. " Or are we about to point out a flaw in someone not present, to make ourselves feel superior? "He only gave the money because he wanted to look good."

If what we want to accomplish is avoid our own annoyance, make someone feel uncomfortable, or assert our ego, we would do well to think twice before suggesting that others change what gives them satisfaction. We can tolerate some inconvenience or inefficiency in the interest of others' self-satisfacion. And when we attribute improper or less noble motives to others without adequate evidence, we reveal our own dissatisfied psyche.

The Truth in Love

But if after our quick motive review we know we have to criticize—and there are times when we do—we can take care to criticize nonviolently. The word "criticize" comes from the Greek *krinein*, which means to judge, or decide. If, out of concern for another, we've decided that something different needs to be done, there are nonviolent ways of communicating our judgment. Nonviolent communication does not shy away from criticizing in this sense of pointing out when something is off the track, when a helpful change needs to be made because what's happening now is hurting the person, or hurting others. An example would be a wife deciding that her husband is drinking too much, or a husband who realizes that his wife is putting on too much weight.

There are times when we have to do what Paul calls "speaking the truth in love" (Eph. 4:15). If a change would be truly beneficial, especially for the other but also for ourselves, then we have grounds to criticize. Maybe a better word than "criticism" would be "intervention." What we are really doing, nonviolently, is stepping in to suggest a more helpful way of proceeding.

When we do intervene, criticize, we should take care to use language that would promote the change, not hinder it by causing the other to feel defensive, guilty, or attacked. One of the most useless observations is, "You made a mistake there" or "You shouldn't have done that." This lays guilt on the person and aggravates him or her. We can't bring back the past. If someone made a mistake, it is futile to reprimand them when the deed is over and done with. Not only futile, but counterproductive. Nobody likes to feel guilty. When somebody does it to me, I look on the person as a manipulator, which inhibits further communication.

Critical Language

Effective intervention does not use command words. "You should stop drinking." "You've got to lose weight." These imperatives will most likely be met with resistance. People don't like to be told what to do, unless they have a masochistic personality that enjoys bowing subserviently. The more normal reaction is drawing back, defending oneself, becoming wary.[1]

"You shouldn't have dropped that dish." It's shattered. Hurt feelings. The child who broke it already feels shame. A nonviolent criticism might go something like, "I really appreciate your helping dry the dishes tonight. We need to concentrate pretty hard on holding on to them when they're wet. How about using two towels, one in each hand? You're doing a great job." That's the "sandwich" technique. It surrounds the suggestion for behavior change with affirmations about the person.

Nonviolent criticism uses a great deal of "I" language. Rather than "Slow down! You're driving too fast," a nonviolent dialect suggests, "I really feel uneasy at these speeds." When we say, "I feel like I'm not being heard," we get the same point across as we do in "You keep interrupting."

A nonviolent "I" statement says something about myself without blaming the other person. It conveys my feelings without holding the other person responsible for them. "I" language shifts the emphasis from their conduct to my experience. It avoids hurting and it gets better results. "I'm allergic to cigarette smoke" is more effective than "You shouldn't smoke in here." When I express how I feel about what's happening, others more often than not will care, and feel drawn to cooperate with me. A constructive change in behavior is more likely to happen when others believe my intentions are not to blame or dominate them.

Shout for Attention

But there are occasions when a nonviolent dialect will call for a deliberately harsh word, a strident tone. Once in a while we need to call attention to something clearly wrong by using language that cuts through complacency. We have to speak sharply, as Paul did with Elymas the sorcerer: "You are a child of the devil and an enemy of everything that is right! You are full of all kinds of deceit and trickery. Will you never stop perverting the right ways of the Lord?" (Acts 13:10). An instant impact is necessary at times.

Several years ago my wife and I were living in Antwerp, Belgium, working at the headquarters of Pax Christi, the international Catholic peace organization. One Sunday afternoon we were walking near the docks and saw, a half block ahead, two sailors stagger out of a bar. One suddenly threw the other to the ground, jumped on him, and began pounding his face. We were horrified. We instinctively began to run up and try to stop them. We had only taken a few steps before a passing car screeched to a halt. The driver jumped out and began shouting something in Flemish. We were sure he was saying, "Stop it! Cut that out right now!" They both looked up. The fighting stopped. The assailant helped the victim to his feet and they both lurched back into the bar together. The driver got back in to his car and left. His shouting had gotten their attention, and stopped the attack.

King used to say that getting people's attention was the purpose of the Civil Rights demonstrations he orchestrated.[2] The demonstrations were in effect saying, "Stop it, stop this segregation!" in a way that caused everyone to listen. Then the dialogue could begin.

Tell It Like It Is

A nonviolent person is concerned with identifying brutality and exploitation for what they are, bring them out in the open so they can be dealt with. Exploiters and brutalizers often try to cover over their terrible deeds with nice-sounding language. The Nazis deliberately developed what they called "language rules" to make genocide less repugnant. They talked about "relocating" to "labor camps" rather than forced deportation to concentration camps. And, ultimately, the mass murders in the gas chambers were called the "final solution." A security officer might speak of "intensive interrogation," when what is really going on is torture. The CIA had a phrase, "terminating with extreme prejudice," referring to assassination of enemy agents.

A nonviolent dialect has a reverse form of such language tricks. It uses forceful, vivid images in order to unmask atrocities, not let them be covered over with deliberately inoffensive terminology. We need to take off the mask, translate the euphemisms into terms of reality. When our military was employing "protective reaction strikes" in Vietnam, dissenters pointed out what was really happening: "Hey, hey, LBJ, how many kids did you kill today?!"

I prefer to call state ordered executions "the death penalty" rather than "capital punishment." The authorities are "killing a prisoner," not just "carrying out a sentence." And I would rather say that abortion destroys a fetus or kills an unborn baby, than that it "terminates a pregnancy" or eliminates the "product of conception." I'd rather call it the "military budget" than the "defense budget." And it's a "hydrogen bomb," on the top of a nuclear missile, not, as military jargon has it, "the physics package."

In one of his first World Day of Peace messages Pope John Paul II wrote:

> Restoring peace means in the first place calling by their proper names acts of violence in all their forms. Murder must be called by its proper name: murder is murder; political or ideological motives do not change its nature...The massacre of men and women, whatever their race, age or position, must be called by its proper name. Torture must be called by its proper name; and...so must all forms of oppression and exploitation.[3]

A nonviolent person not only tries to comfort the afflicted, but also to afflict the comfortable. The intent to speak truth to power is not to cause distress, but to expose the complicity with violence. Exposing violence is a first step to overcoming it.

PART THREE

NONVIOLENCE TOWARD MYSELF

In the process of making our hearts more nonviolent through our speech, it helps to look at those elements in our environment that are upsetting, causing stress, making us irritable, prone to unpleasantness. In being nonviolent toward others in speech and action, we also need to be more nonviolent toward ourselves.

◦ 8 ◦

PERSONAL PEACE

At the height of the Memphis sanitation workers strike in 1968, two young black leaders of a tempestuous group known as the Invaders arranged to meet with Dr. Martin Luther King, Jr. King's aides were uneasy. The invaders were tough, bristling for an argument. But as soon as King appeared, the atmosphere changed. "When he came into the room it seemed like all of a sudden there was a real rush of wind and everything just went out and peace and calm settled over everything," one of the Invaders said later. "You could feel peace around that man. I have never seen anyone that looked like peace, and that man looked like peace. I was kind of shocked."[1]

What King did when he met the Invaders is the effect I'd like to have on others. When I'm relatively peaceful within myself, I can, but when I'm anxious, I communicate my nervousness and people start getting edgy. If I'm calm, it helps others to be calm.

The model that serves best right now is King's image of being *nonviolent toward myself*. I have deliberately tried to cultivate toward myself the same two basic dynamics involved in nonviolence towards others: non-harm, *ahimsa*, and positive personal nurturing.

When I find myself feeling down, I *know* that reaching out to other people can help. It may not be what I feel like doing—I usually want to go away and cope with it myself—but being with others almost always works to counteract my sour feelings and get me back on a more even keel. The helpful, affirming communication I get from others when I'm down helps me get unstuck and feel more able to cope. It has worked well so many times that I go after it now like medecine when I'm sick.

This should not be a selfish proccupation with my own wellbeing, to the exclusion of others. It is rather a conscious effort to take proper care of myself, to deal creatively with what is harmful in my life, to nurture my inner peace.

Stress

Life doesn't usually practice *ahimsa* toward us. We have to help it out. When we are alert to what can hurt us, we have a better chance of warding it off, avoiding being damaged by unnecessary trouble. There is so much stress these days; it can be a nagging worry that discolors our lives, robs us of inner peace, and infects us with higher anxiety. Some of it is a direct result of living in our high-tech, high-pressure society. It makes demands that we usually don't consider violent, but in reality it may cause damage if we don't do something about it.

Inevitably everyone has to face stress imposed by accidents or natural disasters or human perversity—from tornadoes to terrorists, from crashes to cancer. We're better able to handle these if we have learned to deal with the daily stress that pressures us so much of the time.

Buying. Because our national economy is geared to expanding production, we are bombarded with inducements to buy what is being produced, regardless of our means. We easily get entangled in debt, juggling credit card accounts, looking ahead to the next pay check, wondering where the money went, always needing just a little more to make ends meet. "I owe, I owe, it's off to work I go," as the bumper sticker proclaims.

The sheer abundance in our department stores is overwhelming, gagging. If I spend more than a short time in a big place like Sears or K-Mart I feel woozy, off-balance. I experience sensory overload. It's also spiritual overload, because on one level I want what I see, and at the same time I want not to want it. And there's too much there to want anyway. I'm dazed. It's ironic, but appropriate, that our National Product is called "Gross."

I have found that I can only deal with those stores by knowing exactly what I've come to buy, going directly to that department, then getting out as quickly as possible. If I start wandering around, just looking, I begin to feel disoriented. I have to get away from that kind of disturbance, which is a form of violence being done to me. Getting in and out fast is a way of practicing *ahimsa* toward myself.

Automobiles. I also feel stress from some of the machines allegedly designed to make life easier. An automobile provides convenient transportation. But it also breaks down. I don't want a flat tire, a dead battery, or an overheated engine when I'm on my way to teach or to give a talk or catch a plane. I can't avoid these unforeseen irritants altogether, but I try to reduce their likelihood by a few modest measures of preventive maintenance.

When the car doesn't break down it contributes to stress in another way. It's out there waiting to be used, posing the possibility of running more errands, seeing more people, fulfilling more obligations. Sometimes it makes me feel that I should be using it to do something better than what I'm now doing at the moment.

Television. The same with television, a magical show box that provides easy entertainment, especially with the advent of the cable with its dozens of possibilities around the clock. I sometimes wonder whether I ought to be taking advantage of important news programs, or rich artistic offerings, or a never-to-be-repeated nostalgic musical. If I then succumb, I catch myself thinking that I might be wasting time watching television instead of doing something more productive.

I have had to come to terms with television, as well as the car. I try to do that by generally keeping away from both of them. Except when they're *needed*, the television has become a piece of furniture in the living room and the car a decoration in the driveway. I do not turn either of them on except when I decide they're useful.

The Telephone. Another source of stress is the telephone's ring. At the other end might be a friendly voice or some good news. But increasingly often it turns out to be unsolicited solicitations, questions asked, favors requested, announcements of another meeting—more demands on time and energy. It took time to realize that a telephone does not always have to be answered, even though there may be an important call on occasion. For a while my wife and I would switch off the phone's ringing mechanism during dinner. Now, thanks to a brother-in-law's Christmas generosity, we have an answering machine to give us a little relief.

Although they didn't have phones in Jesus' day, I think he recognized this kind of stress too, and tried at times to avoid it. The gospels mention several such incidents. "Because so many people were coming and going that they did not even have a chance to eat, [Jesus] said to them, 'Come with me by yourselves to a quiet place and get some rest' " (Mark 6:31). Those people coming to Jesus probably had genuine needs, but Jesus had to avoid being drained by them all the time.

Work. Anyone's job can be a source of stress. Just holding on to it, in these times of un- and under-employment, is anxiety producing. We want our performance to be up to par, and we worry when we think it may not be. Every job, even the most rewarding, involves concentration on details, much plodding, and dull minutiae. I have found solace in the wisdom of a veteran colleague who once observed, "There's not a job in the world that's not ninety percent janitoring." Or as a successful musician put it, "Genius is 90% perspiration and 10% inspiration." When the work is dull I grit my teeth and get on with the janitoring. I am encouraged by the thought that relief, at least momentary, is in sight at the end of the day.

Relationships. Sometimes an important relationship can deteriorate to the point where we're both being severely harmed. We finally wake up to the fact and admit it, like an alcoholic, whose drinking interferes with daily responsibilities. When we acknowledge being preoccupied with a harmful, even destructive, relationship, that we're becoming listless or frequently bitter, we're like an alcoholic who finally recognizes the problem. Now we have to do something about it. Since others are involved, we need to be sensitive to their suffering, too. Confrontation is always unpleasant, but it may be called for. At least we can withdraw for a while and take a leave of absence to get a better perspective on what should be done to improve the relationship.

Learning to Say No
When I find myself involved in something stressful, I look carefully at it, and unless there are compelling reasons for staying with it, I try, in the spirit of *ahimsa*, to say no. Working without getting enough sleep, taking on one more project in an already full schedule, answering one more phone call—learn to say no.

The trouble is that people interested in a nonviolent approach to life usually have a strong concern for others. They want the world to be a better place, and they're trying to help make it so. They involve themselves in giving; they are often in the helping professions: social service, nursing, religious ministry.

Working with others always raises the stress level. People have needs, make demands, and their problems are usually not simple. Resources are limited, results are imperfect. More needs to be done. Always more. There's so much to do and so little time in which to do it. And it's all worth doing. It's all deserving work. Yes, this meeting is important. Yes, this caller needs attention. Yes, this lonely or sick person needs help. But to be nonviolent toward ourselves we have to choose and we say no to some of the demands. The problem in working toward nonviolence is not that we need encouragement to *do*; rather, we sometimes need encouragement *not* to do. That's hard. It's even hard to think about; it makes us feel a little guilty.

But if Jesus did it, it must be all right. He recognized the need to take a break, to get away. After feeding the 5,000, "he went up on a mountainside by himself to pray" (Matt. 14:23). But it was hard for him to get away. People wouldn't leave him alone. "Jesus left that place and went to the vicinity of Tyre. He entered a house and did not want anyone to know it; yet he could not keep his presence secret" (Mark 7:24). So he sometimes had to slip away, almost furtively, to find the solitude he needed. "Very early in the morning, while it was still dark, Jesus got up, left the house, and went off to a solitary place, where he prayed" (Mark 2:35). He certainly needed the quiet. One evening, after a particularly intense day of healing, "when Jesus saw a crowd around him, he gave orders to cross to the other side of the lake" (Matt. 8:18). He had had enough. He was so tired that he fell asleep in the boat, despite the "furious storm" that came up (Matt. 8:24).

For many of us, as for Jesus, the quiet time we manage to secure is most profitably spent in prayer. For others, it may involve reading, reflecting, or, as it did for King, family life: "On Tuesdays when I'm not out of town, I don't go to the office. I keep this for my quiet day of reading and silence and meditation, and an entire evening with Mrs. King and the children."[2]

The rules of religious orders incorporate times each day for prayer and meditation, to escape from busy-ness for a few minutes and to regain one's focus. The restorative value of this kind of "nothing" time is becoming more and more evident to many people. My half hour of jogging has become an escape time, a focusing time. I consider it a high priority almost every day.

My wife and I decided several years ago that we should take a day off, just to be with each other, to be quiet. When we looked at our calendars, though, we found that the first common free day was two months away! So we reserved it, and tried it out. We decided not to plan anything in advance. That morning when we got up we were a bit anxious about doing "nothing" for a whole day. There were repairs to make, letters to answer, finances to figure. But we had decided to be resolute, to do nothing that seemed like work.

We finally went out for brunch, and then we drove to a park and walked in the woods. It was a beautiful fall day. Another drive, to the Mississippi, where we stood awhile on a bluff, just watching the water flow and an occasional barge labor upriver. A quiet, easy supper at home with no fuss ended our experiment.

It worked! The next day we came back refreshed, toned up, better able to take up the work waiting for each of us. That healing experience led us to try to schedule more of them. We call them our "mental health days."

When we do take the time off, we try to avoid feeling guilty about it. There's so much suffering in the world that if we're going to be effective in reducing any of it we know we must refuse to involve ourselves in all of it. At times we just say no. We're practicing *ahimsa* toward ourselves, which helps our personal peace.

❂ 9 ❂

HEALTHY SELF-LOVE

Nonviolence toward ourselves is more than just trying to keep stress at a minimum. It also means taking positive steps in nurturing ourselves, being concerned for our well-being.

We are born male or female and inherit our genetic traits of height, shape, color; we are of a certain age and inexorably getting older; we have a certain texture to our personality and have achieved a certain degree of intellectual ability. If we don't respect our mind and body with their assets as well as their limitations, we waste precious energy. Such healthy self-love is the foundation of my respecting and loving others.

Caring for Our Gifts

Being nonviolent toward ourselves means taking responsibility for our physical and mental condition. It does not mean pampering or primping, but rather taking care that what we eat and drink is generally healthful, that we exercise sufficiently so that our body functions properly and doesn't deteriorate. Our physical exercise should be in a form we enjoy, like swimming or golf or running, because exercise is hard enough to do regularly in the midst of a demanding schedule, and there is no need to punish ourselves unnecessarily by trying something like weightlifting or Canadian calisthenics.

Nonviolence toward ourselves also includes taking care of our appearance. Gandhi insisted on that. He was always meticulous about his own personal cleanliness, and demanded that those involved in his nonviolent movement be clean and neat, too. He compared it to a soldier, who is required to have every button in place, uniform pressed, boots polished—not because the soldier will be clean and neat in battle, but to foster the soldier's own self-respect and make a good appearance on others. For Gandhi, cleanliness was not a stuffy, middle-class, "respectable" virtue, but an elemental expression of nonviolence. Good appearance is a way of saying that we care enough to make our immediate environment as favorable as possible for ourselves and others.

To help achieve inner peace, it also helps to know how our intellectual ability measures up on a generally accepted scale—our IQ—since it's frustrating to try to change what can't be changed. We should accept the fact that some people are smarter than others, that I am what *I* am with the talents that have been given to *me*. I don't have to be among the brightest, but I should use the intelligence I have.

Accepting our personality profile can also help. Some people are extroverts and some are introverts; some are feelers, others are thinkers. No profile is necessarily better or worse than another. We can smooth out some of our rough edges. For example, introverts can learn the art of conversation, feelers can take time to digest ideas. If we know the basic characteristics of our personality, we won't beat our heads against the wall trying to change the unchangeable. It's what we do with our attributes and faults that matters.

Our Shadow Side

As we know ourselves better, we become more aware that we have a dark side. We recognize that deep down we are capable of shameful deeds, that we actually hurt others. We can flash a hurtful anger, lie and cheat to protect our egos, tune others out with appalling insensitivity, engage in the grossest physical experiences. We can be plagued by a corrosive guilt that makes us want to hurt ourselves or others.

So much violence in our world is the result of not facing the shadow side within us. It's there, straining to express itself. Some people feel weighed down and depressed because they do not face their unpleasant impulses. Sometimes, to counteract these punk feelings, they try to cause someone else to feel worse than they do by making disparaging remarks, by humiliating another, perhaps even resorting to physical or emotional abuse. When they see someone else hurting, they don't feel as bad.

Our shadow side may express itself by projecting some of our ugly impulses onto others, and despise them for having those characteristics. The poison of prejudice is often due to unacknowledged tendencies like cruelty, or callousness, which are "seen" in people of another color, or another religion, or another nationality, whom we then "righteously" despise for their cruelty or callousness as a subconscious way of correcting our own imbalance.

If we are going to be truly nonviolent toward ourselves we must become conscious of our shadow side and come to grips with it. That's not pleasant to do. Who wants to admit being selfish, or indifferent, or cruel? It's a little easier if we can discern something positive in our shadow characteristics. If we consider that our selfishness, for instance, at least prompts us to take proper care of ourselves, it makes it easier to acknowledge it. When we recognize our desire for power, to be in control, we can channel that urge toward the kind of power that helps others and is not just self-gratifying. I can't eliminate my shadow side, but I can recognize its symptoms and try to direct it toward useful goals rather than destructive acts.

Jesus seemed to be referring to our shadow side when he asked why we look at the speck in our brother or sister's eye and pay no attention to the plank in our own (Matt. 7:3). Look inward first, he advised. Fortunately, he didn't say it's enough to look inward, enough to work on curing ourselves. He said we should first take the plank out of our own eye, and *then* we will see clearly enough to remove the speck from our sister or brother's eye (Matt. 7:5). If we come to grips with our own malevolent tendencies first, then we will be better equipped to lessen the amount of suffering in the world.

Creative Worry

Besides taking stock of our own shadow, we practice *ahimsa* toward ourselves by learning how to worry properly. We all hear people say, "Oh, don't worry about that," as though we can just turn it off like a faucet. Well meaning, they would like us stop fretting. But it's hard to take their advice. Until we can come up with a solution to what is bothering us, we can't just stop worrying on the spot.

In fact, a person may be irresponsible not to worry. It may be true that some people worry inordinately, but worry itself can be healthy. It's not true, to paraphrase President Franklin Roosevelt, that the only thing we have to worry about is worry itself. Actually, his dictum, "The only thing we have to fear is fear itself," was not really true, either. It sounded good, but in the dangerous times of World War II there were genuine sources for fear—and people were foolhardy if they didn't recognize them. For all of us at times there really are pressing problems, and we have to be concerned about them to avoid damage to ourselves or others. But we have to worry creatively, not destructively. Those who are blessed with a significant other with whom they can freely share know the relief that comes from just talking about their anxieties. Just talking about them brings some relief—and an occasional helpful suggestion from the other's perspective on the problem.

One way to worry creatively involves setting aside some time each day, a few minutes or a half hour, and spend it on *active worrying*. I do it when I'm jogging, taking a walk, or driving to school. I imagine my mental radar scanning the rest of the day, the time up ahead. When a threat blip shows up, something I feel anxious about—a talk to give, a health problem, not enough money to cover expenses—I concentrate on it and worry about it.

The first thing I do is spin out the scenario: how it could go, what details need caring for in advance, what pitfalls to look out for. Then I imagine a "worst case" outcome. What would happen if things really go wrong—if people hiss, boo and walk out when I am speaking, if a pain in the knee turns out to be arthritis, if the income stopped altogether. I figure out how I would deal with the worst that could happen, which eases the pressure. Then I can go back to thinking how to approach the problem realistically, which is probably not going to become the worst case.

Later in the day, when I catch myself becoming anxious about the same thing, I say to myself, "It's okay now, I've already worried about that. If I have to, I'll take it up again tomorrow. Skip it for now." Sometimes it helps to recall the gospel advice, "Therefore do not worry about tomorrow, for tomorrow will worry about itself. Each day has enough trouble of its own" (Matt. 6:34). My worry time has prepared me for tomorrow. Now let's get on with the rest of today.

This approach usually works. If it doesn't, I sometimes try to imagine a pleasant scene in place of the one that's plaguing me, one of several fantasies in which I'm doing something enjoyable—lying on a beach, feeling relief at the end of a major responsibility, having a good dinner with friends—that help take my mind off the troubling thoughts.

I also find help in the exercise proposed by the Buddhist monk Nhat Hanh:

> Breathing in I calm body and mind,
> Breathing out I smile,
> Dwelling on the present moment
> I know this is the only moment.[1]

Genuinely slow, deep breathing has a physiologically calming effect. Smiling relaxes my facial muscles and contributes to a lessening of my inner tension. And then let go for a moment. Just live in the immediate present. It's really all I've got. The past is gone, the future is not yet.

Buddhists say that when we're walking we should know we're walking, when we're feeling the wind we should know we're feeling the wind, when we're looking at flowers we should know we're looking at flowers—not thinking and worrying about what's going to happen in five minutes or tomorrow. I've found relief in really concentrating for a few minutes on the flow of clouds in the sky. And then I begin to feel refreshed, more lively, more peaceful. I come back with a revived energy.

Optimistic Thinking

A good sign of progress toward inner peace is when we're able to look at what's troubling us not so much as obstacles that oppress, but as challenges to take up. A major difference between an optimist and a pessimist is in the reaction each has to a problem. The optimist thinks about ways to solve it. Pessimists tend to concentrate more on the bad feelings they're having, rather than on what to do to overcome the difficulty.

Psychological studies as well as common sense tell us that when people confronting a predicament believe the outcome will be favorable, they are more likely to achieve a favorable outcome than if they believe it will be bad. Dr. Bernie Siegel, a New York cancer specialist, says that when he has to tell patients they have cancer, he gets one of two reactions. Many respond in despair. "When am I going to die?" Others absorb the shock, then come back with, "What can I do to fight it?" Those who take the latter approach, he found, have a remarkable rate of recovery. The first usually die in a relatively short time.[2]

It's not that everyone automatically becomes an optimist just by wanting to be one. But as we concentrate on life-affirming ways of dealing with the stress around us, taking prudent care of ourselves, affirming our good qualities, and worrying creatively, we find we are moving more in the direction of optimism and gaining inner strength. We are becoming more nonviolent toward ourselves.

PART FOUR

NONVIOLENT CONFLICT RESOLUTION

The more nonviolent we are toward ourselves, the more nonviolent we can be toward others, As long as we interact with people we will occasionally encounter personality conflicts and disagreements. We are especially prone to them if we consistently stand up for our principles, try to act for truth. When we do meet hostility, find ourselves in conflict, we need nonviolent ways of handling it.

10

NONVIOLENT WINNING

I used to play basketball with the kind of intensity a friend called a killer instinct. I was determined to win, and would take advantage of every momentary lapse by an opponent to get a step ahead or muscle my way to the basket. I'm not sure where that drive came from, except that when I was growing up I was strongly influenced by the American ideal of winning.

In grade school I was good at spelling and was often at the head of the line in spelling bees. One time, in the fourth or fifth grade, as I was proudly holding my place at the top against all challengers, I couldn't get the word "lightning" right. I didn't visualize the middle "n." I spelled l-i-g-h-t-i-n-g, and the teacher shook her head. I've always remembered that humiliating walk to the end of the line. When you were at the top and you missed, it was tough.

Ever since then I've remembered how to spell "lightning" correctly. I also intensified my desire to win, to be like Jack Armstrong, the All-American boy. Now, many years and much nonviolent awareness later, that desire has faded. Or rather it's been transmuted into a desire to work *with* others rather than win *over* them. I have a greater sense of accomplishment now when I facilitate a meeting well than when I score better in an athletic contest. I feel I'm a true winner if I help create an atmosphere where others can express themselves, where no one is squashed, where ideas and personalities come bubbling out, but where things get decided, where people leave feeling they have accomplished something.

The basic approach in nonviolence is to be *with* others, not over them or against them. Nonviolence is not a way of putting others down, or getting ahead of them, or achieving a goal at their expense. The nonviolent ideal is to work with others to solve a problem. The idea of winning in nonviolence is changed from winning over *people* to winning over a *situation*.

Competition

The trouble with the usual approach to winning is that it inevitably implies losers. It's a "zero-sum" conflict. I win, plus one. You lose, minus one. The sum is zero. When I'm on top in the game or the championship or the promotion, somebody else has lost the game or the championship or the promotion. As a society we're not very sympathetic toward losers, as I learned graphically in the grade school spelling bee. The humiliation of losing is the other side of the exhilaration of winning.

The American way of winning is institutionalized in school, with honor rolls, curved grading, computer games. It's encouraged by the emphasis on sports—Little League, going after championships, firing losing coaches, winning an Olympic medal. Football legend Vince Lombardi's most famous quote is, "Winning isn't everything, winning is the only thing." Actually his slogan has greater impact when it's spoken than when it's read. It carries a punch. When you look at it on paper it doesn't mean very much, but said out loud, before you have a chance to think about it, it socks out the emphasis on winning.

That emphasis is epitomized by what is becoming our national Holy Day of Obligation, Super Bowl Sunday, where the winners are frenetically acclaimed—and receive the Lombardi trophy—while the losers are left alone to nurse their bruises and wait for next year.

Sports mythology holds that athletics teaches lessons for life. Go after the prize, and go after it hard. Outside of sports, competition is encouraged for jobs, promotions, honors. Win—through intimidation, if necessary. Build a better mousetrap than the other guy, then market it to make a million. Everybody loves a winner.

Some of this is good. Competition can draw us to new heights, stretch our abilities to new levels. But the disdain for losers implied in the American way of winning is contrary to the spirit of nonviolence.

John D. Rockerfeller built a better gasoline business, then made millions by swallowing competitors or driving them out of business. He left many losers in his tracks. The British were big winners in the nineteenth century, when they dominated much of the world. But they created many losers in Africa, and Asia, who were to come back and haunt them in the twentieth century, like the Mau-Maus in Kenya who decapitated English settlers in the 1950s in a bloody prelude to independence.

Gandhi came out of one of those loser people, but he had the genius to escape the cycle. "We don't want to defeat the British," he patiently insisted. "We want them to leave India as our friends." It took decades of nonviolent struggle, but that's what finally happened. The British left India as friends.

In personal nonviolence we put aside the traditional idea of winning, of the zero-sum outcome. One of the early lessons for life I learned from sports turned out to be important for nonviolence, although I had never heard the word at that time. In high school I was not outstanding in sports, no matter how much I wanted to be. But I did "win" my letter in football. In that strange world of adolescent violence, our coach had a philosophy of never cutting anyone from the squad. He made the training and practices so difficult that many boys with dreams of grandeur dropped out. But those who persevered, even though their talent was mediocre, made the team. They won their letters. That football letter was very important to me, because, as I later came to see, it meant winning over a situation rather than winning over people.

Winning With

When my wife and I married at the end of the turbulent decade of the 1960s, it didn't occur to us to approach our marriage in terms of nonviolent winning. We had a more traditional attitude, along the lines of the battle of the sexes: who's going to control this marriage? We each tried to persuade the other to "do things my way."

We consider ourselves fortunate to have come to realize that our marriage itself is more important than either of us getting our way most of the time. We came to find more joy in each other the way we are, with our differences, than in causing each other to change. We learned that, in marriage, when you win you lose. When one spouse wins an argument, both lose something of their shared harmony.

We learned to look on our marriage as a partnership, a cooperative venture, a common effort. When there are chores to be done—cooking, cleaning, the finances—it doesn't matter who does them, as long as they get done, and as long as one person doesn't always do the more unpleasant ones. We try much more now to respect each other's unique gifts and insights, and, yes, to back down at times in the interest of the long-range gain in our relationship. We have found that the key to nonviolent winning in marriage is power *with*, rather than power *over*.

Nobody deserves to become a loser at my hands. What I'm after is behavior that is assertive rather than aggressive, that steps forward but doesn't step over, that moves ahead *with* others rather than ahead *of* them.

As I learned more about nonviolence I began to see that even competitive sports can be approached with a cooperative attitude, concerned to help others achieve something worthwhile in the experience. Now it doesn't matter so much if I win a contest on the scoreboard. What does matter is that I get some exercise, and that all of us enjoy the game.

People play competitive sports to achieve something: to enhance their courage, sharpen their skills, display their prowess, or just to have fun. We enjoy winning, especially when we're good at the game. In competing nonviolently we don't have to forego this enjoyment, but we should not take getting the best score too seriously; we should play the game so that everyone enjoys it.

Competing nonviolently never means deliberately losing in order to allow the opponent to avoid feeling humiliated. That would be a patronizing gesture that would cause greater humiliation later on when it's found out.

Because the other side may not be looking at competition the way we are, we will often be involved in a unilateral approach when we engage in it cooperatively. That's one of the attractive aspects of nonviolence; we have the power to alter any situation regardless of what the other side does. We can inject feelings of respect, consideration, moderation on our own. If the opponents misread us and mistake moderation for weakness, we can correct their perception by our non-defensive firmness—joined by a show of respect for them as persons.

The Trap

Achieving cooperation while working for mutually agreeable outcomes is not as easy as it sounds. Our egos bruise quickly. Even if I tell myself over and over that I want to be nonviolent, that I want to win *with* others rather than *over* them, just let the game start or the conflict erupt, let unpleasant words be spoken or a sneer be perceived, and I feel a familiar surge of self-protection. I want to defend myself and show them I'm not going to take it, not going to be abused. I want to get back at them, then get ahead of them.

As soon as these feelings emerge, we're at the first critical point for nonviolent winning. We have to recognize what's happening and put on the brakes. We have to stop the situation from deteriorating, which will happen if we follow our hurt feelings.

Someone accuses me: "You had no business making that remark. It was completely out of line." That hurts. I want to defend myself. "Of course I did. It was the truth." The other person, who has suddenly become my opponent, persists. "Your remark was insulting and stupid." I feel further attacked. "Who do you think you are, talking to me like this!"

Violence breeds violence. Hurtful words evoke hurtful words.

As another sports-inspired axiom has it (or perhaps it's war-inspired), the best defense is a good offense; that is, when we're attacked, we defend ourselves best by counterattacking. But it doesn't work that way. The best defense in an inter-personal conflict is not a good offense. When we counterattack we stir up more resentment in our opponent, who is then pressed to strike again, to intensify the attack. The best defense to a verbal sting is not a counter-sting, but a patient waiting for the attack to simmer down. It requires a show of self-possession, self-confidence, perhaps humor, an ability to rise above the fray.

The best defense is a careful movement in the direction of nonviolent winning. The very first thing to do when someone speaks unpleasantly to us is *Don't respond in kind*. As soon as we feel that urge to defend, we have to say to ourselves very firmly, "Hold back. Wait a minute. *It's a trap*." If I say what I'm feeling, I'm going to get myself in deeper and be sucked into a conflict I really don't want. Things will get worse quickly, so don't say it.

Holding back like this is not at all passive. It takes control, self-discipline, to keep those feelings—which we undoubtedly will have—from spilling out. This is what King meant when he said that nonviolence is ultimately the way of a strong person. The strength he was talking about is not physical, but interior. It's a strength of mind, of will, of soul.

A friend of mine is a language instructor at the Federal Prison in Memphis. One particular inmate was known for his abusive language to the guards. Usually the guards would shout back at him, then punish him by denying some of his privileges. This only made the prisoner angrier. One day he accosted the language teacher, and poured out his abuse. My friend just put up his hand in a "stop" gesture. He said, "I'm not taking this. You're going to have to carry it around yourself the rest of the day." The prisoner stopped, and looked dumfounded. He never again spoke disparagingly to my friend.

This holding back, this controlling our reaction, is the first step in breaking the cycle of violence, all kinds of violence. The battered child of yesterday easily becomes the abusing parent of tomorrow, when the cycle is not broken. The teenage Palestinian girl slapped by a gun-wielding Israeli soldier will want to find a gun for herself—unless someone can help her find another way.

Unless it's broken, the deadly cycle goes on, as in the case of the man in Arkansas who killed fourteen people, most of them in his own family, around Christmas 1987. His explanation was, "I've gotten back at everybody who wanted to hurt me." He was hurt, he felt very bad, so he struck back. For him the best defense against the hurt was a good offense, the best he knew: Kill them. The violence came full cycle back to him when he was sentenced to be executed for his crime.

For a nonviolent person the trick is, *Don't fall into the trap*. The nonviolent person does not take the bait, does not get caught up in damaging language or actions when the other side is using them. This takes a quick, firm decision: Hold your tongue. Don't do anything.

Assertion

Restraint is only the first step. Nonviolent winning takes positive, patient action. It involves putting ourselves forward rather than holding ourselves back. When I participate in a conference or a meeting, I often look for an opportunity to make an early intervention and "get on the scoreboard." In asserting myself at the beginning I start to create an atmosphere of respect. Later on, when significant questions are up for discussion, what I say might be received as a genuine contribution.

Assertion means, "Here I am, I have some ideas, feelings, and abilities that might help, and I'd like to share them." We can be assertive when we feel we have power, the self-confidence to put ourselves forward when we think it will do some good. It is different from aggression, which is also self-expression—but in a way that hurts or represses others.[1] What we put forward in nonviolent assertion should be based on truth, truth in the Gandhian sense of something conducive to the well-being of others as well as ourselves. We are not assertive merely to toot our own whistle, to show off our abilities, but for the sake of something good that can come of it. The key to nonviolent assertion is a sensitivity to others—that they're with us as we put ourselves forward.

It is important to evaluate the people we encounter as we assert ourselves with nonviolence. We may find we're up against a *forcer*, a person who adopts a power-oriented style. Forcers want to prevail and will push hard for their position. They listen very little as they try to steamroller us. Their manner often crosses over from assertion to aggression.

Another style that's less pushy, but more difficult to work with over the long haul, is the *passive-aggressive* response. Those who interact this way do not actively put up resistance, and may even seem to agree with us. But they tenaciously hold their original position and try to get their way through sullenness, procrastination, or inefficiency.

We also have to look out for someone who is overly *accommodating*, always seeming to be ready to agree. That's too easy. It's not right. The person's ego may be so weak that the normal give and take of conversation, and life, are threatening. Accommodators avoid conflict whenever possible, and if they have to engage in it, they look for quick compromises that do not really satisfy either side.

The assertiveness that leads to nonviolent winning is like a dance. It's different with different partners. It suggests and responds in different ways to different kinds of people. For example, the forcer may in fact really be after the good feeling that comes from seeing others capitulate. If we show a forcer that we respect the ideas and opinions being expressed, and, more importantly, the forcer's *self*, we will be better able to get on with the task together than if we react in the same slug-it-out style.

The passive-aggressive person needs much attention and care, and painstaking attention to detail. As each obstacle is thrown up, we need to deal with it carefully, assiduously avoiding anything that will be taken as a personal attack. After awhile, as our concern is perceived as non-threatening, we can be on our way toward a solution that satisfies both of us.

We have to watch not to take an accommodator lightly. Giving in to us quickly may not be a sign of genuine agreement. Asserting ourselves before such a person can cause immediate withdrawal, which is not conducive to a winning outcome in the nonviolent sense. When we see this happening, we have to back off, and move very gently, tentatively, bringing the person along with us.

The fundamental principle in nonviolent winning with people of all types is that *Nobody wins until everybody wins:* wins something, at least; wins whatever is valuable in the position initially held; wins respect; wins the acknowledgment of one's fundamental dignity.

◉ 11 ◉

COOPERATION AND TRUST

Gandhi insisted that truth—and nonviolent winning—requires concern for *genuine* human well-being. When the British were clinging to their imperial sway over India, he knew that their conduct was not in their true interest. He felt they had to change, to see things differently—for their own sake, as well as for the people of India. By his assertiveness, always gentle but always forceful, Gandhi helped them see things in a new light. He let them know he always respected them personally while he helped them through the unpleasant process of conversion. They eventually found it to be true, that they were better off relinquishing their colonial hold over a distant people who wanted to be free.

Like Gandhi, we have to be careful, solicitous even, of our opponents' well-being. What we seek is not to suppress conflict, but to transform it into an encounter in which both sides benefit. We want to turn competition into cooperation.

Negotiation

King used to say that the main objective in the demonstrations he led in cities across the South was to create a climate in which the civic leaders would be prepared to negotiate.

Nonviolent people believe that words are more powerful than weapons. Words reach the mind and heart of our opponents and help them change from the inside. When we fight back physically or emotionally, we try to force them to change from the outside. Change that comes through dialogue is likely to be deeper and last longer than change brought about through force.

We have all experienced that intent dialogue can change the way we look at things. As Schillebeeckx has pointed out, after a particularly significant exchange of words people feel themselves touched, buoyed up. "They have discovered a new world, and even the very objects around them seem changed."[1]

This happened to the man who had forced a woman into a deserted building where he raped her. As he was leaving, she called out, "God will forgive you." What she said at that disturbed moment pierced his heart. He began to feel remorse there and then. He went back to her, broke down in tears, and apologized profusely. When she accepted his offer to get her a cab home, he even gave her money for the fare![2] Words from a self-possessed, caring person can work wonders.

Words are the medium of negotiation, which is at the heart of nonviolent action. Negotiation is the real guts, the inner workings, of nonviolence.

The process leading to nonviolent winning (for both sides) is a give and take, sometimes a long, drawn out effort to understand and to respond. We listen carefully to what is being said, we try to discern how strongly the other side's ego is tied to the position being advanced, and when we propose our own beliefs, we employ all the nuances of the nonviolent dialect.

Several years ago the Peace and Justice Center in Memphis was creating a slide show for a national organization. After working on it for months to get it into shape, we sent it to the commissioning group for a reaction. Several days later the Director of the Center told me, crestfallen, "They didn't like it, and they're not going to pay us for it." Having been recently immersed in negotiation theory, my first thought was, "Let's not take this as a final rejection, but as the first stage in negotiation." He agreed to try again. Several phone calls later we found out the problem areas, set about changing them, and within months the slide show was accepted—and paid for.

The first time my wife and I had our income tax audited, we reacted the way most people do when they receive the notice—afraid that the government would find all kinds of flaws, and that we would end up paying a lot of money we didn't have. Then it dawned on us to treat the audit as an exercise in nonviolence. We would be very conscious of *ahimsa* in our dealing with the auditor, trying to avoid any defensiveness that would make him more severe in his findings. We would communicate our respect for him as a person doing his job, careful to avoid any self-righteousness or moralizing. We would also maintain our position about the deductions we claimed, and admit our ignorance of the intricacies of the tax laws when we had to. We would be politely assertive. And we would be realistic in expecting to have to pay something to justify the government's expense of having an agent spend a considerable amount of time with us.

When the auditor came to our home, he made it clear that he knew we had withheld part of our tax as a war protest. We let that go without comment. Instead, we talked for a while about his family, children, church, career. We gave him an opportunity to decide that we were not going to be personally difficult. He commented on our peace banners and mementoes. "Oh, you do that kind of thing, too."

When he examined our records, we expressed what we had done in a way that communicated a respect for the regulations he knew so well, while disagreeing over how much of our money is spent on military violence, while the government is not taking adequate care to meet the human needs in our country.

Our nonviolent approach to this audit was worthwhile. The results were much better than they might have been. Although we did have to pay a few hundred dollars because he disallowed several deductions, he not only accepted the vast majority of them, but even spent considerable time helping us rearrange our tax return to give us advantages we didn't know we could claim. His advice provided us with a model that has served us well with the IRS since. We could not detect any insincerity in his repeated affirmation that he enjoyed working with us.

In the negotiation process minds will be changed. We'd like to think the auditor changed his image of tax protestors, and we came to appreciate a hard-working accountant who was doing his job steadily, willing to go out of his way to help us. If the outcome is a true nonviolent win, the parties will have positions at the end of the process different from what they were at the beginning.

Unpleasant Change

But change, even for the better, is an unpleasant process. Although we appreciated the IRS agent as a person and gained valuable experience about the audit process, we did not want to lose the money we had to pay. Britain finally became friendly with India, but for decades the British resisted leaving, considering it an unthinkable humiliation and loss. Most whites in Birmingham and Memphis and other southern cities felt disturbed and insulted when the social fabric of their cities was disrupted as Martin Luther King, Jr., led the civil rights marches in the 1960s.

The disturbance we cause when we are nonviolently firm poses a theoretical problem: When we put ourselves forward, we are initially throwing up a block to someone else; we are saying, in effect, "You can't have what you want right now, because I'm here with my position, which is different from yours." Initially, the frustration we cause by our firmness is a kind of pain, and since the first principle of nonviolence is *ahimsa*, non-harm, we feel uneasy about causing others to be disturbed by our stance.

But pain is not always the same as harm. A dentist causes pain in filling a tooth. A surgeon causes pain in removing an appendix. A teacher causes pain by insisting on work outside of class. The frustration we bring about in a nonviolent encounter can be a healthy prelude to moving a situation forward, to exploring a new idea, to strengthening interpersonal skills. Nonviolence does not seek to defeat or humiliate, King said, but to win an opponent's friendship and understanding. Even when the nonviolent person has to be firm about something that disturbs the other, that disturbance is not what is finally intended. It is merely a "means to awaken a sense of moral shame in the opponents," if that is necessary to move the process toward truth. "The end is redemption and reconciliation," he insisted,[3] reconciliation in the sense not of reverting to the status quo, but of moving on to a higher level of harmony than when the confrontation started.

Trust

In order to create a cooperative atmosphere in any competitive situation, we have to start with a degree of trust. We don't have to like the other person—the tax auditor, the sheriff with the dogs and firehoses, the British soldiers in India. Trust has nothing to do with liking. It has everything to do with expecting a certain kind of humane, rational behavior.

Government leaders repeatedly tell us that we don't have to trust the Soviets in order to sign arms control treaties with them. They insist that our "national technical means" of verification, especially our surveillance satellites, can reveal any cheating the other side might be tempted to do. The agreements don't rest on trust, we're assured, but on verification.

But this is not really true. The whole Mutually Assured Destruction system of nuclear deterrence is based on trust—a real trust that the Soviets will act rationally, that they will decide not to use their nuclear weapons against us because they know they will be destroyed in turn if they do. We have no way of assuring their decision, no national technical means of enforcing it, but we trust them to make the right descision because we believe they will act in the way that's humane for their own people.

Trust covers a wide range, from the initial expectation of rational behavior to the confidence of a loving response from someone with whom we've shared a life. The trust appropriate for nonviolent engagement is the very first stage. It is not a sentimental letting down of our guard, making ourselves vulnerable because we feel we ought to be nice. Trust in nonviolence means believing the other side to be rational; it means starting out by assuming the other will act decently. In the beginning, therefore, we don't put up our defenses, scowl, tie on the gloves. We start out, rather, by communicating an attitude of openness. We are not intimate yet, and perhaps never will be. But we are realistic. We know the dangers, the risks, but we're going ahead anyway.

On a visit to New York I had to take the subway early one Sunday morning. Downstairs at the station I found myself alone execpt for two young men, late teenagers, fifty yards away, cavorting noisily and erratically. Otherwise the platform was deserted. I thought about trust, and I thought about prudence. I decided to stay within sight of the agent in the ticket booth as I waited for the train, which seemed to take forever to come. When we all got on the same car I nodded to the young men in a way I hoped was sufficiently pleasant for New York. Nothing else happened. I trusted, but only at the beginning level.

The alternative to trust is to assume at the outset that the other side is going to pursue its self-interest at our expense. If we start with this attitude we will have our defenses all the way up. On the subway platform I would have been perhaps looking for a way to call the police. Or I may have left and decided to take a taxi instead.

From the point of view of being somewhat safer from an initial attack, that subway distrust would have made sense. But that's the short-range view. We know enough of the dynamics of attack and defense, the aggression-counterattack spiral, to realize that distrust, as soon as it's perceived, is bound to contribute to a deterioration of the encounter.

Should the other side mistake our trust for weakness and move to take advantage of us, that's when we become quiet and firm, when we control our retaliation reflex and stop ourselves from becoming defensive. We continue to trust as we become assertive in whatever way the encounter calls for. Eventually, we hope, the other side may come to realize that lowering their own guard and getting on with our mutual business is in their interest as well as ours. This is what our trust should lead to. It reduces the psychological pressure the other side feels from us, and helps create an atmosphere in which they can think of alternatives to aggressive behavior, alternatives that move the encounter more in the direction of cooperation.[4]

A Verbal Attack

Let's see how these theories play out in a conflict most of us get involved in at one time or another.

At work, with colleagues around, you see a supervisor approaching rapidly with what looks like fire in the eyes. Trust, you tell yourself, trust in rationality, in basic human decency, trust that this is going to work out all right somehow. Coming up to your desk, the supervisor says in a loud voice, visibly angry, "You've just made a big mistake. You insulted an important client, and you've lost thousands of dollars for us."

Your first reaction is defensive. You want to say, "I don't know what you're talking about." Or, "I didn't do anything like that." You want to protect yourself. Or you might even want to strike back. "What do you mean, you've made a lot of mistakes, too, that have cost us plenty of money."

But then you recognize that such a response is a trap and you immediately hold back. Keep quiet. Don't take the bait. Don't say anything right away. You look at the supervisor, attentive, waiting. He continues, still angry, "How in the world could you do something so stupid!"

Now if there's one thing you know, it's that you are not stupid. Eleanor Roosevelt once said that nobody can make us feel inferior without our consent. That helps. You're not consenting. You also know that when you are being attacked verbally, you have to size up the situation quickly. Is the attack based on truth? Better to acknowledge the mistake than to fight back defensively. Is it based only on partial truth, but represents the antagonism or the frustration of the attacker? Then the mood of the attacker is what we have to deal with, at least as much as the substance of the attack.

But it's hard to keep all that in mind when you're being criticized. You feel a little flustered. Everybody's listening. You've got to say something. So you use the question technique, trying to learn what's really going on, giving the supervisor an opportunity to ventilate if that's important, and giving yourself a chance to pick up clues about feelings. "I'm not sure I understand what you're getting at. What happened?" You try not to inject a note of hostility into the question, and you phrase it in a way that doesn't insinuate anything improper in the supervisor's approach. You're using the nonviolent dialect.

"You know what I'm talking about. That man who came in here this morning and had his car towed away. You insulted him. And now you should call him and apologize."

Now you remember the incident in question. While you were just beginning to talk to a client you happened to look outside and see a Mercedes recently parked in one of the handicapped slots. A few minutes later you saw it being towed away. You remarked, not knowing whose car it was, that you appreciated the security people being prompt in removing cars that had no business in the handicapped places, especially high priced cars whose owners could afford to pay for parking. The client looked startled, you remember, then jumped up and ran outside to try to retrieve his Mercedes. That's the incident in question. Yes, partial truth. You may have made a mistake in stereotyping a Mercedes owner and letting it out.

But right now you must lower the emotional tone. So you say, as quietly and straightforwardly as you can, "I think I know what you're referring to, that man whose car was towed away. What did he say?"

And so the story is spun out. More quickly, now, and a little more calmly. It becomes clear that the Mercedes owner let out frustrations over his lost car by making you a scapegoat. It also becomes clear that your supervisor needs to express some frustrations over our lost client by laying you out in front of your colleagues.

At this point you have kept quiet long enough. Now you must say something; not to communicate is to communicate. You can't let the supervisor interpret your silence as admitting the charge of stupidity, or as being intimidated by his attack.

You know what you shouldn't say: any of the emotionally charged words that have already been used: insult, mistake, money lost. You shouldn't say, "I didn't insult the guy." That only repeats the charged word again and lodges it more firmly in everyone's mind. So you acknowledge that you did say something to a client about a car being towed away, and that perhaps you were out of line by injecting a personal prejudice into a conversation with a stranger. In reacting this way, you are trying to respond to the supervisor's need to feel in charge, while not escalating the confrontation. You are also trying to uphold your dignity with your colleagues and not give the impression that you are beaten or assenting to an exaggerated charge. You try to let them assess the supervisor's behavior as well as your own.

If your first responses aren't effective, if the supervisor is still angry and continues to attack you, you can resort to *metacommunication*—saying something about the process of the discussion rather than about the subject of the discussion. "I'm having some trouble with this conversation. We can't seem to get together on it. I don't want to make things worse. Could we talk about it in your office?"

Fortunately, you don't have to resort to it this time. Your earlier response works. The supervisor calms down; his need to assert authority has been satisfied. You maintained your self-control and acknowledged whatever truth there was in the attack while not escalating it. You showed respect by not counterattacking, and you maintained your dignity and self-possession before your colleagues.

You both win, nonviolently.

Right Perseverance

If the conflict had become prolonged, you might have been tempted to give up, to skip it, agree, walk away, or try to convince yourself it wasn't important. But we shouldn't give up too quickly. The sixth step on the Buddha's Eightfold Path is right effort, or, as it's sometimes translated, right perseverance. It's important to maintain the effort, stay with the job, complete the project, try again for a nonviolent win over the situation.

If an argument deteriorates into personal acrimony, with no glimmer of light, we might have to terminate it by withdrawing, at least for the time being. But if we keep a nonviolent spirit throughout the effort, our opponents will often develop a new respect for us, even if they are not persuaded to our cause. When someone says, "I don't agree with you, but keep it up. We need people like you in the world," we know we have won something. Gandhi was right when he said we always win when we fight nonviolently.

PART FIVE

NONVIOLENT RESPONSE TO ASSAULT

Even though Gandhi said we always win, at least something, when we engage in a conflict nonviolently, it's hard to see how we can be nonviolent in the most difficult and dangerous conflict we can face outside of war: an assault on our person. We need to look at the problem of physical assault very carefully, because if we can respond nonviolently to this, we will certainly find lesser conflicts easier to handle.

12

PERSONAL ASSAULT

I've never been mugged—at least not yet. I have often thought, though, about what I would do if someone jumped out of the shadows with a knife and demanded my wallet. Or if that pair of teenagers on the isolated New York subway platform swaggered over and asked for twenty dollars. Or if when I was stalled on an empty freeway a car suddenly pulled in front of me and the driver stepped out pointing a gun.

I don't know what I *would* do, and I'll never know until something like that happens. But right now, when I can think about it coherently, I know what I would *like* to do: remain calm. I would like to save my life, of course, and avoid whatever would trigger violence in my assailants. I would want to do whatever would defuse the confrontation and turn it around.

Like automobile accidents, fires, tornadoes, and earthquakes, the possibility of personal assault is a fact of life today. We are all potential victims of a sudden attack on our persons, our possessions, our life. Everyone should be prepared to face it.

Conventional wisdom says that if we can't get away, we

should either submit or fight back strongly. "Save your skin." Self-preservation is nature's first law, we're told. Get by with the least damage to ourselves. An empty wallet is better than a slit throat. Losing one's virtue is better than losing one's life.

Or we are advised to use force, if possible. A Memphis police lieutenant who runs clinics on how to cope with rape gives this advice: "First, try to escape or scare away the assailant by wrenching free or yelling. If the criminal doesn't let go, then you have to either give in, or hurt him in the most effective and efficient manner possible." This means gouge out an eye. Kick hard at the groin. Shoot, if you have a gun, and shoot to kill. His advice has a point for people not sensitive to nonviolence or not practiced in its ways. Essentially he offers the two traditional modes of survival in time of danger: flight or fight.

If we really believe, however, that active nonviolence is an effective alternative to flight or fight in other areas of life, we need to explore how we can respond nonviolently in this most critical of all personal dangers, when an assault occurs. Here are some true stories about people who were not experienced in nonviolence, not committed to *ahimsa*, but who did just the right nonviolent thing at the right time.

Three Events

A woman with two children in a disabled car late one night on the New Jersey turnpike looked up to see a man pointing a gun through her window. He ordered her to let him in the car. Instead of panicking, she looked him in the eye and, like an angry mother, commanded, "You put that gun away and get in your car and push me to the service area. *And I mean right now!*" He looked startled, put the gun away, went back to his car, and did as she ordered: pushed her car to the service area.[1]

A colleague of mine walking late one winter afternoon was jumped by two young men hiding in bushes under a viaduct. They demanded money. He said he didn't have any. They began punching him, repeating their demand for money. He felt helpless and didn't know what to do. Then it flashed into his mind to call for the only assistance he could think of. He rolled his eyes and started shouting, "Jesus, help me. Jesus, help me!" They stopped hitting him and looked at him as if he were crazy. Then they ran away.

A lady drove into the parking garage of Memphis's largest hospital one afternoon to visit a friend. As she eased her car into a space she noticed a strange-looking man lurking nearby. No one else was in sight. She usually kept a gun in her glove compartment, she said later, but that day she had left home without it. She had to think fast. She got out of the car, and as the man came over, she looked squarely at him and said in as firm a voice as she could muster, "I'm so glad there's a man around. Could you walk me to the elevator?" He replied meekly, "Yes, ma'am." She thanked him, got on the elevator alone—and practically collapsed out of fear and relief.

Although none of the three people were committed to nonviolence, they had improvised what we recognize as a truly nonviolent response. They did not act like victims. They engaged the potential assailants as human beings, and in two of the incidents managed to evoke a sense of decency that resulted in their being helped rather than hurt.

Since we are faced with the possibility of being subject to assault—I prefer to say "subject to" assault rather than "victim of"—there is much we can do nonviolently to keep ourselves from becoming victims.

Prevention

It is very nonviolent, not to mention practical, to do everything we reasonably can to avoid being attacked in the first place. That includes locking doors, walking with others rather than alone, avoiding high risk areas, and being alert to potential danger wherever we are. We have to be, as Jesus said, "shrewd as snakes" while we're being "innocent as doves" (Matt. 10:16).

For a person tuned in to nonviolence, prevention is not being cowardly, but realistic. We are not helping ourselves or any potential assailants in the vicinity by naively thinking that everything will be all right all the time. Out of *ahimsa*, the desire for non-harm, we need to avoid making ourselves easy objects for attack. We should not tempt others to attack us.

If we see an attack coming, we should avoid it or seek cover. A woman in Hungerford, England, who was at the scene when a gunman began firing his rifle at marketplace strollers, killing 16 people, said she survived because she "dove for cover."

At critical times like that we should dive for cover, too, if we can. We need feel no compunction about it; Jesus himself frequently took evasive action. After a verbal confrontation with some of his adversaries, "they picked up stones to stone him....Jesus hid himself, slipping away from the temple grounds" (John 8:59). That was his way of "diving for cover." Another time, right after John the Baptist was killed, "When Jesus heard what had happened, he withdrew by boat privately to a solitary place" (Matt. 14:13). He could feel the pressure, and knew that his time had not yet come. He fled the scene.

He advised his disciples to do the same thing: "When you are persecuted in one place, flee to another" (Matt. 10:23). Stay away from troublesome areas. Don't make yourself an easy mark. When Jesus sensed danger, he hid out and tried to evade it as long as possible without giving up his commitment.

Our safety precautions send a strong signal to anyone who would do us harm. It is not that we are scared, but that we are alert and prepared to take care of ourselves. Two strange men entered an aerobics class in which my wife was participating and began talking loudly, distracting the exercisers. No one knew what they wanted, but they seemed capable of creating mischief. One of the exercisers went over to speak to them. He told them quietly how serious the class was, and that anyone who wanted to take part had to sign a waiver form and pay a fee. They were welcome to join if they wanted. He didn't accuse or threaten; he just spoke straightforwardly, matter-of-factly. They listened, saw his seriousness, then turned away and left the room. No trouble. It was an exercise in prevention. Jesus would have approved.

Restraint

If we are up against an attacker who is crazed by drug or drink, or who is schizophrenic, or temporarily insane, nonviolent human interaction is nearly impossible. If we have the opportunity, restraint may be our only recourse.

One man told me about his wife who had been mentally ill. She would fly into rages. "I looked into her eyes, and it seemed like she wasn't there," he said. She would scream and curse and throw things and was incapable of listening to anyone. She refused to see a doctor or do anything to help herself. Then one night, in one of her fits, she took a knife from the kitchen and started toward their child's bedroom. "That was the end of the line," he said. "I had to stop her." He bounded across the room and, as gently as possible but as firmly as necessary, he wrapped one arm around her from behind, grabbed the wrist of the hand that held the knife and squeezed until she dropped it. Then, still holding her, he dialed the emergency telephone number and waited for the ambulance to take her to the hospital. He said it was the hardest thing he ever had to do in his life.

When I think of restraining somebody nonviolently, I would like to do it as strongly and effectively—and as lovingly—as that man did his wife.

Self-Possession

As a remote preparation long before any attack occurs, we can sharpen our ability for an effective nonviolent response by increasing the power of our personhood. We belive that we are important, we are valuable and we want others to believe it about themselves. We are not victims; we are not cowering and cringing before life's challenges, fearfully looking over our shoulder to see what might be pursuing us. We stand straight, eyes calm, alert, moving ahead. We walk confidently, not with cockiness, which is a way of compensating for insecurity, but in a straightforward and open manner. We are not rash or brash; we don't take unnecessary risks, blind to danger. We are who we are, and we present ourselves to the world that way.

The caricature of the swaggering sheriff with a pistol strapped on one side, a heavy flashlight on the other, a billy club dangling from his belt, so loaded down that he walks with his elbows pointed outward, is the image of a fearful man, so lacking in self-confidence that he needs all this hardware to protect himself.

If we are so dominated by fear that we arm ourselves to hurt those who would attack us, we have sunk to the level of the assaulter. We have become like the enemy in our desperation to overcome the enemy.

In principle, people committed to nonviolence don't carry weapons. It is because we believe in *ahimsa*, but it is also because we believe that in a crisis our personal ability is more effective than a gun. Our only weapons are the ones described by Paul as the "armor of God": "Stand firm, then, with the belt of truth buckled around your waist, with the breastplate of righteousness in place, and with your feet fitted with the readiness that comes from the gospel of peace" (Eph. 6:13-15). Truth, righteousness, and readiness are powerful nonviolent weapons. Armed with these, our personal power increases.

These weapons, more than guns and knives, have a deterrent effect on a would-be attacker. Think of a robber lurking in a doorway late at night watching potential marks approaching down the street. The robber will want to pick out those who look like easy victims: timid, uncertain, fearful, unprotected. Someone who appears in command, confident, will not be as appealing a target. If I am this person, I'm likely to be passed over in favor of an easier target (and I'll probably never know how close I came to being attacked).

A large-statured friend of mine, a long-time peace activist, wasn't passed over once. In a small town in South Dakota, on a sidewalk in full daylight he was suddenly faced with a much smaller man flashing a knife and demanding money. My friend, who had very little money anyway, said that the first thing he thought of was the incongruity of their sizes. "All I could do was laugh," he said. He didn't feel any fear, although later he said he was surprised he hadn't. His self-confidence was deep. The assailant glanced up at him, looked puzzled, then turned and ran away.

If an attack does occur, this kind of self-possession, this awareness of our personal power, this confidence in our nonviolent armor, is the foundation of defense. But it's only the foundation. An understanding of what is likely to happen and some practice in nonviolent techniques can give us a truly effective defense against personal assault.

◉ **13** ◉

DYNAMICS OF A NONVIOLENT RESPONSE

Before we look at what we can do nonviolently if an attack does occur, a preliminary word is crucial. Anyone who has been victimized by a personal assault should in no way feel guilty for not having responded in the nonviolent way described here. The trauma of being attacked, of being personally violated, is a painful burden to carry. If it happens, we do the best we can at the moment. We may not do the best we could if we had complete control of ourselves, but when we're attacked we don't have complete control. It's sudden—there's no time—the attack is strong, brutal.

We imply no judgment on anyone's past. We are trying to prepare ourselves for effective responses in the future. The point of this examinination of nonviolent possibilities is not to intensify past problems. The consequences may not be past, but the event itself is. We were who we were at the time. But now we've moved on, we're different, and we're learning something new.

Perhaps if we are attacked again, we would do something new, and the outcome might be different because the kind of nonviolent response we are looking at now really is new. It is new in that we are focusing powerful ideas about human beings and human conduct on the problem of what to do when we are personally attacked. It is new in that we are combining the findings of sociology and psychology with the experiences and insights of the twentieth century prophets of nonviolence, and creating new ways of handling ourselves when faced with a powerful threat.

The Attacker's Mentality

Here is one person's description of how he felt during a murder he committed. He wrote it from prison in a letter to a friend of mine.

> I'm a very peaceful person unless I'm pressured to a point where no one will help. I'm only human, and a human being can be pressured to do things, especially if you're weak and have drug or drinking problems. I've had such a rough childhood I go to pieces when grownups intentionally try to hurt me. Your intention may not be to murder, but then you get provoked. You just no longer have any control, and you go into a rage. It's too late when it's done. Now I'm considered some kind of animal, which I'm not. I just had a problem and no one would help, so I went crazy on my mother-in-law and father-in-law. Enough about this. I get in a state of mind thinking about it, and then I can't sleep for days.

Experts tell us that most people who commit assaults are fearful and probably angry at the forces in life that have wounded them, like this man in prison. One study of juvenile offenders found that the more violent ones came from violent environments: 75 percent had been physically abused by their parents and 70 percent had seen extreme violence in the home. They are familiar with patterns of violence and, when pushed, resort to the same patterns themselves. They are "broken" people.

Cruelty is a complex of fear and anger. People who have

themselves been hurt often seek to humiliate others in turn. They need victims of their own. They welcome a show of fear in others as a sign of powerlessness which, by contrast, heightens their own sense of strength.

It takes a great act of faith on our part to believe this of the person about to assault us. We have to go beyond appearances, like knowing the earth is round no matter how flat it looks. We *know* an assaulter is in all probability a fearful, broken, weak person, no matter how threatening, aggressive, and powerful he or she appears at the moment.

Our Reaction

Basically two dynamics can come under our control in an assault. The first is our self-possession, the way we see ourselves and carry ourselves. The second is our part of the interaction with the attacker, what we do, and what we say. We can't control what the attacker does, but we are in charge of what we do in the face of the attack.

Our normal response to an assault attempt will probably be fear at first. We are confronted with a threat, a forceful presence, a fearsome expression, a total stranger perhaps with a weapon suddenly invading our vulnerable space, demanding that we do something very unpleasant. We may find ourselves feeling disgusted with what's happening, and getting angry at the one making it happen. But above all we are fearful that we will be hurt or killed.

We know we have to be very careful. We can't appear to stall, or be cute, or frustrate the attacker, who is bound to be edgy and in a hurry to get it over with.

If we have any time at all to think, and if we're schooled in nonviolence, our mind will tell us that the attacker, unless insane or under the influence of drugs, is capable of a human response to human overtures. Our mind and training will also tell us that it is precisely in making those overtures, guided by our sense of self-worth and personal power, that we have a chance for an effective reaction.

Thinking about it now, before any incident, we *know* this, although when it happens we will probably *feel* very frightened. We *hope* that the nonviolent understanding clicks into place in our mental system, that it overrides the fear quickly enough for us to do something constructive. If it does, we have a chance for a creative response.

What to Do
In reality, we may not have a chance to do very much at all. The attacker may be in such a hurry, in the grips of another fear, that it's over almost before we knew what hit us. But if we have the opportunity for some interaction with the attacker, the key is to remain calm. A sudden move will be taken as threatening and the fear we feel as weakness. It will help to take a deep breath, then look the person in the eye to pick up some clues, to size up the situation right away, almost intuitively. If the attacker is armed and seems nervous, about to panic, we may have to hand over wallet or purse without further ado. But perhaps we might be able to do more. Let's think it through in theory, ahead of time.

As the attacker sees it, I, the intended victim, might hit back; he is prepared for that. That's the purpose of the knife, or gun, or the surprise jump out of the dark: to overpower me and prevent my fighting back. If I do fight back, I give the attacker justification for using the weapon. By resisting in the way he anticipated, I provide moral support and strengthen his attitude.

The attacker is also prepared for a show of fear; it is what he expects and hopes for. Both responses, fight and fear, immediately reassure him that things are going as he has anticipated.

But suppose we do the unexpected. We don't fight back, and don't show any fear. We may feel it, but we do not show it. We show respect (we are not being irrational), but no fear or ugliness. We don't appear threatened ("Get in your car and push me to the service station," said the women on the New Jersey Turnpike. "Right now.") And we don't appear threatening. ("I'm so glad there's a man around to walk me to the elevator," as the lady in the hospital parking garage had improvised.)

Usually we won't have an effective nonviolent response figured out ahead of time; it will be spontaneous. One morning a young woman was returning to her car in a library parking garage. A man who seemed pleasant approached her and said hello. She nodded back to him. She was just about to open her car door when he grabbed her arm roughly. She immediately shook him off, looked at him squarely, and said, "You gotta be kidding." He was startled and let go. She quickly got in and locked the door. He looked at her for a moment, then walked away. Her sense of personal power was so strong that it overrode her fear. She reacted naturally, her assailant was thrown off guard, and she was safe.

If an attacker starts out feeling contemptuous of the intended victim, those feelings become suspended because of the not-at-all-victimlike reaction. They are replaced by the beginning of wonder, of uncertainty. Suddenly the attack not going according to the script; it's not cut and dried any more. It has become an open-ended process of interaction. In this kind of exchange, a nonviolent person has a definite advantage. We usually know ourselves better, we're more confident of our ability to reach out helpfully, we understand better the possibilities inherent in the interaction.

Such a person is a friend of mine, Maggie Pharris. She has studied the dynamics of nonviolence and has tried to put it into practice in her family and professional life. It has given her the ability to respond nonviolently in times of crisis. One such time happened in Minneapolis. She has told this story on television, written about it, and has helped others gain courage from learning what happened to her. One evening she was going for a run after work when out of nowhere appeared a wild-eyed man who grabbed her by the arm and pinned her against a tree. She looked at him, and saw panic in his eyes. After a tense moment she said, "Let's get away from the street. If anybody sees us here there'll be trouble." He was surprised. "What are you doing?" She told him that she could see by his eyes that he had experienced a lot of pain, and that he didn't need to be hurt any more by getting involved with passers-by. Even hurting her wouldn't do anything but add to his pain. She suggested they sit down and talk.

This, she said later, was the turning point. She could feel a change in his attitude. Her first reaction had been an overwhelming sense of fear, of being blocked. Then, just as suddenly, in a flash she realized that if he started to molest her there, and someone else had come along, things would only have got worse. Others beside herself would be hurt. Once she was able to feel something other than her own fear, she was free to take the initiative.

She instinctively knew she couldn't break his hold, knew too that screaming would only infuriate him, and that arguing, trying to "talk him out of it" would be absolutely futile. So she acted on her long familiarity with nonviolence by speaking to him quietly, directly, human to human. "Let's get away from the street. If anybody sees us here there'll be trouble."

When she looked at his eyes, she said, she was actually able to feel a sense of sorrow for him. She didn't oppose him or try to get him to let go. "Let's get away from the street." He also wanted to get her away from the street. But she had reached him on her own initiative. That was the key. His scenario began to break down. She had sparked a human response. Now *he* was doing what *she* asked, walking away from the street, sitting down, and talking for an hour and a half. It turned out he was a Vietnam veteran who had frequently acted as an executioner killing many people in the war, mostly civilians. Before that he had had a rough childhood, and was currently out of a job. He was, Maggie said, "a very, very broken person."

It was now dark. She finally felt the tension had subsided sufficiently that her danger from him was much less. But she still didn't feel free to leave. So she asked him to walk her home. The next day she found flowers at her front door with a card, "Thank you for being my friend."[1]

Maggie responded to her attacker with all the skills she had mastered in her nonviolent training. At this difficult moment her preparation brought out the very best in her.

Moral Jiu-Jitsu

By refusing to act out the attacker's scenario we offer some resistance, but it's psychological, not physical, resistance. This is less threatening, and if we do it right, it's even somewhat soothing in an atmosphere that is hyper-tense. We start to play a new tune, suggest a different act in the play. The purpose is to tone down the climate of hostility and begin replacing it with a sense of security, sympathy, and good will. As the exchange goes forward, the attacker ideally will begin to calm down, as Maggie's did. The desire to take advantage of us will diminish in the face of the gentle pressure we exert. On the one hand, we show respect for the attacker as a person, do nothing threatening, and implicitly acknowledge the attacker's dignity. At the same time we refuse to cooperate in the attack.

A half-century ago Richard Gregg, one of the early theoreticians of Gandhian nonviolence, described this process as "moral jiu-jitsu." The nonviolence and good will of the potential victim act in the same way that the lack of physical opposition by the user of physical jiu-jitsu does, he said, causing the attacker to "lose moral balance." The attacker "suddenly and unexpectedly loses the moral support which the usual violent resistance of most victims would render."[2]

The attacker plunges forward, as it were, into a world of new values, feeling insecure because of the novelty of the situation, unsure of how to handle it. Poise and self-confidence diminish. The intended victim not only does not fight back, but even pulls the attacker forward by kindness, openness, and, if necessary, a willingness to suffer, so that the attacker loses moral balance. The nonviolent person, "knowing what is happening and having a more creative purpose, keeps moral balance," Gregg went on. The nonviolent person "uses the leverage of a superior wisdom to subdue the rough direct force of the opponent."

Once we understand the dynamics of a nonviolent response, see how it can work, and above all see some people for whom it has worked, we have a better appreciation of its power for our own lives if we are ever faced with that awesome opportunity.

14

IT CAN WORK

When I shared stories of nonviolent resistance to assault at a workshop, one woman said of the people who had successfully evaded the attacks, "They were just lucky." They were lucky in hitting on just the right thing to say, just the right look or movement, and just the right susceptibility in the attackers. They were lucky to get out of it alive and intact.

They were lucky in the same way that a soldier who survives combat is lucky. The bullets just didn't find him; he managed not to trip off any land mines; when the bombs fell and the shells exploded he was lucky to find protective cover. But that soldier increased his chances of surviving by going through rigorous training. He had practiced crawling on his stomach with live ammunition whistling overhead; he learned how to dig himself into the ground; he felt the earth shake when bombs exploded around him. Above all, he learned to discipline himself, not to panic, to rely on the protection of his unit, and how to improvise under fire. He was lucky to survive. But if he hadn't been trained, his chances of surviving combat would have been much worse. He might not have been so lucky.

The same is true with a nonviolent response to assault. Any time we get through it without damage we are lucky. But we increase our chances for a good outcome by training ourselves, by studying and practicing what to say and how to act.

Practice

We should not think that a nonviolent response to assault will be automatic, that merely knowing about it will cause us to react correctly when the time comes. Instead, we need practice. Like a soldier getting ready for combat, we need to go over the moves.

We need, first, to go over the moves mentally, imagining what we might do in different circumstances, how we might react, and how we would like to react if we're suddenly faced with a gunman demanding money. A man in New York who works for a peace organization knew the dangers in riding subways. He used to think about what he would do if confronted with an assault. He decided he would throw out his arms in an open gesture so they would see he wasn't armed or threatening, and he would say he didn't have any money. Sure enough, it happened on a subway platform as he had pictured it. A man confronted him with a knife and demanded money. He had gone over the scene so many times in his mind that his response was almost instinctive. He threw out his arms and said he didn't have any. The assailant stopped, looked at him intently, then said, "Okay," and left.

One occasion for practice are the "little rapes" or street hassles so many women are confronted with at one time or another. Using a nonviolent dialect and some of the techniques for nonviolent winning can help gain valuable experience that will stand in good stead when faced with more serious threats.

The closest we can come to actually practicing what to do in an assault is to get together with others and role-play possible scenarios. In that way we get the feel of how to react, and we learn how some things we say diminish the hostility and others don't. Role-playing is the only way short of the actual experience itself to find out what we are likely to do, what we can do.

Pax Christi USA, the American section of the international Catholic peace movement, has developed a training program for nonviolent response to personal assault. It is the only program of its kind in the country that I know of. Over the period of a weekend, led by a skilled trainer, participants have the opportunity to simulate, practice, and discuss various scenes of assault, learn how they felt when being "assaulted," discover more effective ways to deal with it.[1]

A young participant gave her verdict of the training workshop after it was over.

> This is such a relief. I've been to those sessions where the police showed us how to defend against rape, and I came away really upset. I was afraid it might happen to me, and I know I couldn't gouge out someone's eyes if it did. Now I can see that there are all kinds of different things that I can do, nonviolently. And I don't feel so afraid any more.

Beyond Pragmatism

Of course, a nonviolent response, even with the personal power of self-possession and skills honed through practice sessions, doesn't always work. But neither does a violent response. There is a risk in choosing to defend ourselves nonviolently, but there is a risk in whatever we do when faced with assault. There are no easy answers. A positive, nonviolent response has at least as much, and most probably more, chance of successfully evading an assault than a violent response does.

We're heartened by that prospect. But even though pragmatic calculations can enhance our commitment to nonviolence, it is not really based on them. The basis of nonviolence is our respect for the fundamental dignity of every human being, including the person who is threatening to assault us. The police officer who advised potential rape victims, "The most important thing is for a person to get through the ordeal alive and uninjured," articulated the cultural value of self-preservation above all. By contrast, for the truly nonviolent person, the main concern is that *both* parties, not just the one being attacked, get through the ordeal alive and uninjured—physically, mentally, morally.

While it is certainly not healthy for us to be assaulted, it is also not healthy for the one who would perpetrate the assault. In responding nonviolently we try not only to prevent it from happening to ourselves, we also want to *prevent the other from committing it.*

The positive steps we take nonviolently are for our own good, but they are also for the good of the attacker. Christians have a specific foundation for taking them, "the mind of Christ" (I Cor. 1:16). Paul said that our "attitude should be the same as Christ Jesus" (Phil. 2:5). Christ's "mind," Christ's "attitude" was clearly expressed in his law of love, and particularly in the most demanding clause of that law: love of enemies.

Anyone who assaults me is at that moment very much an enemy. This is one of those times when I clearly have an enemy, a real, palpable, threatening enemy. Paul pointed out that we are called to be reconcilers because we are "in Christ," we are part of a "new creation; the old has gone, the new has come! All this is from God, who reconciled us to himself through Christ and gave us the *ministry of reconciliation*" (II Cor. 5:17-18).

To love our enemies, and to seek reconciliation does not necessarily mean that we feel affection toward them, but that we want life for them, we want wholeness, we want *both* of us to get out of this ordeal as well as possible. This spirit takes us beyond pragmatism. I'm comforted to know that nonviolence will probably work, but in any event, we know that our desire for the attacker's good as well as our own is the "mind of Christ," and that in operating out of it we have that cosmic companionship to which King referred.

We may not, and probably will not, always achieve this ideal. Nonviolence is an experiment and we are on the road to it. We may not get there every time we're faced with a crisis. We may act spontaneously and fight back. But because on the spur of the moment we have hit or kicked—or killed—an assailant to protect ourselves, or given in out of fear because we couldn't do anything else doesn't mean we will act the same way the next time. We may not—we probably won't—always reach the nonviolent ideal, but we know it's there, a shining star worth pursuing. We hope and pray that we have the love, faith, and courage to continue to pursue it.

PART SIX

NONVIOLENT PUBLIC RELATIONS

The more we use nonviolent techniques and see that they work, the more likely we will be to respond nonviolently when someone really does threaten our life. We can help prepare ourselves for that crunch by trying to be a nonviolent person in everything we do, especially in those daily encounters that comprise our "public relations."

• 15 •

COURTEOUS ASSERTION

In Antwerp, my wife and I found people who would respond pleasantly to a nod and a smile, despite the language barrier. We had to be careful not to appear as happy-go-lucky Americans insensitive to traditional Belgian ways. Recall the scene in *Crocodile Dundee* in which the hero, whisked suddenly from his native Australian bush into midtown Manhattan, greets everyone on the street exuberantly, and the harried New Yorkers look at him like he's crazy.

Anyone committed to nonviolence will try to take local customs into account. Such signs of respect and responsiveness to other human beings make everybody feel better. It is gentle, courteous assertion; it is simple courtesy and elementary politeness. It may stem from a motive no more profound than a desire to make our human dealings more congenial. Yet it can also be a natural extension of personal nonviolence. Out of respect for others and for ourselves, we want to avoid many of the little hurts that dot the day. In the spirit of nonviolence we can reach out with a helping hand or an affirming remark. We can look on every human encounter as a possible exercise in positive nonviolence.

"Public relations" here does not mean the organized effort by advertising experts to persuade people to have positive feelings toward something. "PR" in this sense often seems contrived, putting on a good face no matter what lies underneath. In personal nonviolence we strive for authenticity, not appearances. We want to be genuine with the people whose paths cross ours—checkout clerks, mail carriers, the person ahead of us in line, the driver in the next car at a stop light—even though we're not going to be deeply personal with them.

I-You

The Jewish philosopher Martin Buber described two ways of relating to others. One he called "I-Thou," a deep, personal sharing with those to whom we feel close. The other he called "I-It." That's where we keep people at a distance and treat them impersonally.

Harvard Divinity School professor Harvey Cox suggested a third category, appropriate for those we meet occasionally but with whom we are not intimate. He called it the "I-You" relationship. We are pleasant, helpful when necessary, but not intimate. He saw the Good Samaritan as an example of an I-You encounter. "The man who fell among thieves was not the next-door neighbor of the Samaritan, but he helped him in an efficient, unsentimental way," Cox wrote. "He did not form an I-Thou relationship with him but bandaged his wounds and made sure the innkeeper had enough cash to cover his expenses."[1] The Good Samaritan did what had to be done to assure the victim's health and well-being. Then, presumably, he was heard from no more.

This is an apt description of nonviolent public relations. We look at people as a friendly "You" rather than an intimate "Thou" or an impersonal "It."

Boston Globe columnist Ellen Goodman has lamented the decline of what she called "civility" in our hectic society. "The dozens of daily encounters between strangers who pass each other on the sidewalk, buy from each other in the stores, deal with each other crossing streets and boarding buses have indeed become lean and mean," she wrote. "Most of us look away when we pass strangers. It is the exceptional person who stops to help the woman maneuvering her kids and groceries up the staircase. We rarely give up our place in line or on the subway....Drivers who won't give each other an inch happily give each other the finger."[2]

If civility is indeed declining in our society (and not just in Boston), we who are trying to be more nonviolent can restore some of it by being courteous and polite in these daily encounters. We leave a little of it in our wake as we sail through by treating people as "You's" rather than "It's."

When people leave a store or an office in the South, they invariably hear, "Y'all come back." This is a harmless, pleasant, and civil way to end a transaction. It can be an act of genuine personal nonviolence if we think of it in those terms.

Nonverbal Communication

Another aspect of courteous assertion is our body language. Experts suggest that as much as 70 percent of the information passing between two people is communicated nonverbally. It pays to pay attention to the way we comport ourselves. Folding our arms can be taken as a protective gesture, indicating that we're holding ourselves in and putting up a barrier. Slouching may appear to be a sign of disrespect, even if we don't mean it that way and are only trying to be comfortable.

Making someone look up to talk with us can be intimidating. I remember my first visit to a doctor's office. I was placed on a low sofa in front of his towering desk. "Now, what seems to be the problem?" I was not inspired to seek treatment from him.

Ahimsa encourages us to make our nonverbal signals—gestures, tone of voice, posture—as non-threatening as possible. For instance, I try to be conscious when meeting small children, to get down to their level or raise them up to mine. A tall adult can seem overpowering to a child. I've found that when the two of us are on the same level physically the little one becomes much more responsive.

We can also be careful about invading personal space. In our culture, people tend to feel uncomfortable when someone comes very close, within about two feet. When anyone does it to me, I feel the need to back away. So I try to be conscious of not pressing in on others too closely.

I try to be conscious of the relative position I take when talking with someone. The straight ahead stance, face to face, has been called the "challenge position." When I'm talking with someone for more than a minute or so I try to take a more supportive stance, facing at a slight angle. The subliminal message is that it offers an escape route. It tends to make people a bit more relaxed, less confined, less threatened.[3]

Eye contact is another important nonverbal signal. If I don't give enough eye contact I will appear evasive. On the other hand, too much can be intimidating. When someone continuously looks me in the eye, staring steadily, it's unnerving and makes me feel uncomfortable. A relaxed and steady gaze, looking away occasionally, is a more nonviolent approach. And if eye-to eye is uncomfortable, we can focus on another part of the person's face, the forehead, the mouth.[4] Looking directly, especially when the other is talking, shows our interest in what the person is saying, another way of being courteously assertive.

Nonviolent Driving

The way we drive is also part of our nonviolent public relations. The same fundamental approach holds here as in other areas of life. We respect others and don't want to offend them, so we're courteous. At the same time we respect ourselves and don't want to be run off the road, so we're firm—gently, respectfully, but definitely.

We drive crisply, straightforwardly, ready to yield out of courtesy, but taking the initiative when it doesn't offend. The same idea that makes us not want to appear as victims to a potential assaulter is operative here. We don't want people to take advantage of us. It is not good for them, psychologically and morally. It's better for others to respect us as we respect them.

In driving, as in response to an assault, we need to be conscious of prevention, so we drive defensively. We delay a few seconds before starting on a green light, in case someone on the other street is running the red. We are alert to other cars changing lanes suddenly, without warning. Defensive driving is essential, especially in this age of hurry, of people rushing about their own business, sometimes creating a cocoon inside their car with windows up and the radio blasting.

We drive defensively, but we don't drive with defensiveness. That's different. Defensiveness takes place when someone tries to cut in front of us and we hold our position without yielding to show them they can't do that to us. Defensiveness is when another driver shouts at us because we made a mistake or got in the way, and we shout back to maintain our self-righteousness. Defensiveness is when we're piqued by the antics of another driver and we lean on the horn to show that they were wrong. The nonviolent driver has enough self-possession to absorb unpleasant antics without reacting with defensiveness.

The way we drive, as with our other public relations, can be a genuine expression of our commitment to nonviolence.

16

FRINGE BENEFITS

In the effort to be nonviolent in public relations, Jesus did not rule out some self-interest. If we avoid offending, we lessen the chances of being offended ourselves. If we reach out to help, we increase the chances of getting help ourselves when we need it. "Do not judge, and you will not be judged. Do not condemn, and you will not be condemned. Forgive, and you will be forgiven. Give, and it will be given to you. A good measure, pressed down, shaken together and running over, will be poured into your lap. For with the measure you use, it will be measured to you" (Luke 6:37-38).

If we are committed to nonviolence when the chips are down, we should be willing to accept suffering rather than inflict it. It is encouraging to realize from time to time that practicing nonviolence can carry personal rewards. We are not called to unnecessary unpleasantness.

Humor

A nonviolent person has to face heavy issues, such as torture and nuclear terror. It helps immeasurably if we can cultivate a sense of humor—not about torture and terror, but about ourselves and about life. Nonviolence need not be equated with grimness. All through his life Gandhi loved to laugh and make others laugh. He graced difficult circumstances with his sense of humor. He loved jail, he once said, because it gave him a chance to catch up on his sleep![1]

People like to laugh. We can help them by an occasional sparkle. "One nuclear bomb can ruin your whole day."[2] Or, "I can stand anything but pain," as my favorite philosopher Oscar Levant used to say. Humor can create a mood in which positive and beneficial emotions, such as zestfulness and hope, can emerge. It brightens people's outlooks and spirits. It's a way of being positively nonviolent toward them in a helping, affirming way.

Laughter has a healing quality, physically as well as socially. Thanks to some interesting medical experiences, we are becoming aware scientifically of what our common sense has told us all along: it's healthy to laugh. Norman Cousins, the former editor of *Saturday Review*, in a remarkable little book, *Anatomy of an Illness*, relates how he was healed of what he was told was an incurable disease, *ankylosing spondylitis*, by laughter therapy—deliberately spending time each day in his hospital room watching Marx Brothers movies and reruns of *Candid Camera*.

He had to demand this for himself, asking friends to bring him a movie projector and the films. He felt better after ten minutes of hard laughter than after all the pain-deadening medicine he was taking. Gradually he cut back on the medication. After some weeks he was discharged from the hospital, cured.

In Los Angeles, the Hospital Satellite Network has produced a television service called *Patient America*, specializing in humor for hospitals. It consists of classic comedies and other entertaining features, and is available not only on patients' television, but in some surgical recovery rooms.

Healing humor is one of the fringe benefits of personal nonviolence.

Laugh at Ourselves

There is a mean kind of humor that pokes fun at others, or points out their flaws. It is a form of defensiveness, a shield, the "good offense" that some adopt to protect themselves. One of the signs that we are making progress toward inner peace is when we can laugh at ourselves rather than constantly feeling the need to defend ourselves.

It takes inner strength to hold myself up for humor, rather than others. When I can laugh about something that otherwise contributes to anxiety—such as growing older ("I find myself paying a lot more attention to sunsets these days"), or losing some agility ("I'm about to forget jogging and take up power walking")—it's as if I were saying to myself, and to others, "If these traits are funny, they can't be so terrible." Only when we are comfortable with our flaws, when we have accepted ourselves as imperfect, can we dare expose them to our own and to others' laughter.

When I hold up something personal for laughter, I realize that trait is probably present in others, too. The public display of my imperfections encourages them to identify with me in a safe way, as they see that I not only have a particular flaw and can talk about it, but can even laugh about it. If they see me laughing about something they don't like in themselves, it helps them face it, too.

When we laugh at ourselves and invite others to do so in a healthy way—not in a self-degrading put-down—we deter them from making hurtful fun of us. They are less likely to make jokes at our expense if we are already making jokes about ourselves. Thus, we lessen the incidence of personal affront, reduce the times when we feel down because others put us down, and diminish the stress from unpleasant human encounters.[3] It's another fringe benefit of our nonviolent public relations.

The Small Stuff

One purpose of nonviolent public relations is to create a favorable impression in order to help counteract people's negative feelings about our unpopular stands on larger issues: disarmament, peace in Central America, racial harmony, overcoming sexism, ending apartheid. This struck me for the first time when I was marching in a peace demonstration in Baltimore in 1968, at the height of the Vietnam War protests. At that time the Baltimore police were involved in a dispute with the city government over a salary increase. Someone among us began a chant, "More pay for cops!" We all took it up whenever we saw police on duty during the demonstration. We waved at them, and almost always they smiled and waved back. I didn't feel emotionally involved in the economic plight of the Baltimore police at the time, but I was gratified that they seemed less hostile toward us because we showed concern for them.

Whenever the Nuclear Train with its load of hydrogen bombs came through Memphis, our peace community would hold a vigil by the tracks. We always took care to notify the authorities of our intentions well in advance of the train's arrival. It was almost always expected in the dark, cold depths of the night. A contingent of police would invariably appear, "for your own protection," they said, but also to arrest us if we interfered with the passage of the train. Some in our group made it a point to go over to them and strike up a conversation. We wanted them to understand what we were about, that we were not hostile to them, but were terribly concerned about this train transporting its deadly cargo through the heart of our city. We wanted good relations with the police and wanted to avoid any misunderstandings or unnecessary prejudice on their part. They might not agree with what we were doing, although several voiced their own misgivings at the danger the train posed to the city.

In times of social stress, a favorite tactic on the part of many who would uphold the status quo is to accuse peace and justice people of being disorderly, dirty, ignorant, or incompetent. This is a good way to arouse public sentiment against our cause. If we take pains not to offend in these lesser details, we remove these excuses and keep the focus on the main issues.

This is what Jesus did, I think, when he complied with the Temple tax. "After Jesus and his disciples arrived in Capernaum, the collectors of the two-drachma tax came to Peter and asked,

'Doesn't your teacher pay the temple tax?' " (Matt. 17:24). Jesus considered himself exempt from that tax. But it wasn't an issue he wanted to engage in. So he said to Peter, "So that we may not offend them, go to the lake and throw out your line. Take the first fish you catch; open its mouth and you will find a four-drachma coin. Take it and give it to them for my tax and yours" (Matt. 17:27). He wasn't about to get sidetracked from his Kingdom mission by a dispute over a relatively minor tax assessment.

A college student put it succinctly for me a few years ago: "Don't sweat the small stuff." But don't back down on the big stuff, either. We need to hold firm on the larger, more important issues, even if it means causing upsetment. Jesus did say, "I did not come to bring peace, but a sword" (Matt. 10:34), by which he meant "division," as Luke interprets his saying (Luke 12:51). When the chips are down and a big issue is on the line, such as nuclear disarmament or the abuse of children, then we stand up for what is right, no matter whom we have to offend, no matter what divisions we cause.

We are more apt to be effective on the big issues if we don't offend on smaller matters, like a temple tax, and if we are careful to make our public relations nonviolent every day. The fringe benefit then becomes the main prize.

PART SEVEN

A NONVIOLENT LIFESTYLE

Keeping our eyes on the prize means not getting sidetracked by trivia. Those of us who are not hermits constantly meet with trivia. It is easy to get caught up in the swirl of feeling that we need more—or better, or different—clothes, cars, food, furniture, gadgets. In a society flooded with consumer goods, a society whose economy is predicated on growth—not enough but more, always more—people who would be nonviolent need to reflect from time to time on their lifestyles. We need to become aware of the trivia, and keep it in its place.

○ 17 ○

TO LIVE DECENTLY

Friends of ours had welcomed into their home an 18-year-old girl from Nicaragua, who had come to study at a North American university. Her trip to Memphis was the first time she had ever been out of her country. A few hours after she arrived her host family took her with them when they went grocery shopping. After they had been in the supermarket for a few minutes, the girl began to feel nauseous. She became pale and had to run outside the store. Afterwards, when she calmed down, she tried to explain what had happened to her. The overwhelming abundance of food was such a contrast with the bare shelves in Managua that she became ill.

When I visited Nicaragua, I saw those bare shelves and experienced the absence of basic goods, like soap and sugar. Now, when I go into a supermarket, and I'm flooded with all kinds of products, I often think of that Nicaraguan girl. We have so much, while they have so little.

When I'm bombarded with television commercials to make me attracted to this new car or that brand of potato chips, or when I start on the Sunday newspaper and have to wade through dozens of ad supplements to collect the reading sections, I'm annoyed—more at the gross overabundance portrayed than at the unwanted interruption.

I've been around long enough to see through those ads. Billions of dollars are spent every year to manipulate me to buy things, most of which I don't need: wine coolers, a camcorder, a compact disk stereo system, or instant grits. I'd like to think I'm immune to it, but the incessant presence attracts my attention more often than not anyway.

Affluence and Violence

To be personally nonviolent we have to resist cultural pressures for violence. It's also important to stand firm against the cultural pressures for affluence. The two, not surprisingly, are connected.

Not long ago I participated in a conference on death and dying. A Navy officer was giving his rationale for participating in the death-dealing which is war. "We have to defend our standard of living against those who would take it away," he said. "You mean," asked a lady incredulously, "you would go to war to preserve our electric toothbrushes?" "Well, no," he answered so sincerely and straightforwardly, "but I would go to war to preserve our right to use electric toothbrushes." He saw the military's purpose as protecting our consumerism, our "right" to have whatever we wanted, no matter how trivial, and no matter what the consequences were to anyone else in the world.

There's a clear psychological connection between affluence and violence. When we have what others lack, and when we think they might try to take away what we have, we lean toward using violent measures to protect our possessions. I saw a bumper sticker recently that proclaimed, "God, guns, and guts made America great. Let's keep all three." The right to have whatever we want spurs people to buy a gun to protect their homestead, their possessions. And as a matter of fact the same desire to have whatever *they* want drives predators of those possessions as well, would-be thieves and robbers who go after a piece of the pie.

According to French philosopher Jean-Paul Sartre, that connection exists in all societies characterized by what he calls "scarcity." Where some people lack resources the society considers important, that society is charcterized by a climate of violence. A nonviolent person striving for *ahimsa* has to disengage, at least emotionally, from the consumer ethic that fosters conspicuous consumption while millions suffer from the lack of necessities.

When my wife and I visited Yugoslavia a few years ago the family with whom we were staying announced proudly, "We're now as good as you Americans. We have everything you have." They meant cars, homes, clothes, good food. Actually it wasn't quite true; their standard of living was considerably below what would be considered middle-class here. But I was sorry to see that their vision in life was so narrow. Emphasis on affluence is always inward turning, self-centered, generating the willingness to exploit others if necessary to get what we want.

Affluence around the world is usually gained at the expense of poor people. Every baseball used in the major leagues is manufactured in Haiti where the women get ten cents from Rawlings or Wilson for each ball they hand-sew. They can make $2.00 a day doing this—when they can get the work. And most can't, in that poorest country in the hemisphere.

But a job like stitching a baseball for ten cents carries some ambiguity with it. As the Prime Minister of Singapore once said, he'd rather have his people earning $2.00 a day making something for an American company than earning nothing as they would if the American company weren't there.

Yes, something is better than nothing. But what needs to be changed is an international economic system that fosters exploitation in the Haitis and Singapores of the world. The system itself is a form of violence to the people it keeps in economic servitude.

Amusing the Well-Fed

The nineteenth-century Russian writer Tolstoy, whom Gandhi considered his mentor, suggested that "Love for humankind won't let us serve it by amusing the well-fed, while leaving the cold and hungry to die of want." The contrast between Tolstoy's "well fed" and "the cold and hungry" is startling evidence where the Third World touches on the First. I've crossed the Rio Grande from El Paso into Juarez, the second largest city in Mexico. Within several blocks of the bridge I've driven on badly paved streets, seen poorly clothed children, felt the press of crowds of sad-eyed men and women. From the perspective of relatively affluent El Paso, it's no wonder the narrow, shallow Rio Grande is bounded on the U.S. side by a sturdy, tall, chain link fence for miles in either direction. Keep them out, the fence says forcefully, or they'll flood over the border like an army of hungry ants, snatching whatever they can from us.

We don't have to go to El Paso to see the same contrasts. Down the block, or across town in any large city, we can see rundown neighborhoods, people out of work idly keeping each other company, long lines waiting for surplus cheese, the Third World in our midst.

Conditions like these make us uneasy, even angry, and dissatisfied with the present economic system., which is a form of violence. We disavow it as we disavow all violence. But what, concretely, can we do about it? How can we live nonviolently in a world of economic violence? There is no easy answer. Nowhere in the world do we see a larger society that has solved these problems. Models are scarce. The socialist countries proclaim a vision of economic and social equality, but the hard realities in every one of them make us wonder whether they are even on the right course.

We can decide to leave the present system entirely, adjourning to a remote plot of land where we grow our own food and make our own clothes. We can unite with other people and try to create a new economic order for ourselves and our little group where we live.

If we choose not to drop out like that and are still committed to a greater degree of nonviolence, we have to make some basic decisions about our lifestyle. How are we going to live in what Gandhi called the *himsa*, the harm-causing, of the present economic system?

Neither Poverty nor Luxury

In looking with a nonviolent eye at the economic spectrum, we can be sure that, from a Christian as well as a common-sense point of view, the poverty that exists at one end of that spectrum is not good. It is not a characteristic of the Kingdom of Heaven, the Reign of God. In that Kingdom the hungry will be fed, the naked clothed, the homeless sheltered. We help to bring it about by following Jesus' suggestion: "Sell everything you have and give to the poor" (Mark 10:21). Share with others. If someone is hungry, *feed* the person. Make people less poor. Poverty—a degradation of the human condition, something to be eliminated—is not right. No one should be poor.

The luxury, the superfluity at the other end of the economic spectrum, is not right either because of the selfishness it inextricably involves. Also, it is not right because it is inevitably gained at the expense of some other people somewhere. Pope John Paul II pointed this out in his encyclical, *Sollicitudo Rei Socialis* (On Social Concerns): "Huge sums of money, which could and should be used for increasing the development of peoples, are instead utilized for the enrichment of individuals or groups."[1]

Jesus makes the same point in the parable of the rich man and Lazarus (Luke 16:19-22).

> There was a rich man who was dressed in purple and fine linen and lived in luxury every day. At his gate was laid a beggar named Lazarus, covered with sores and longing to eat what fell from the rich man's table. Even the dogs came and licked his sores. The time came when the beggar died and the angels carried him to Abraham's side. The rich man also died and was buried. In hell, where he was in torment, he looked up and saw Abraham far away, with Lazarus by his side.

Jesus does not say why the rich man went to hell, giving no details of his former life. The implication, though, is that he was condemned because, living in luxury, he ignored the poor beggar at his gate. He maintained his luxury at the expense of the suffering of others.

Decent Living

There's a large area between the extreme of poverty at the one end and the extreme of luxury at the other. I think of that large middle ground as "decency." That is where people who would be nonviolent need to locate themselves. Anyone may be forced by circumstances into deprivation—in prison perhaps, or caught in a catastrophe such as an earthquake or a tornado or a war—but if we have the ability to regulate our lives, we would opt for decency rather than misery, or luxury.

Decency means that our basic needs of food, clothing, and shelter are met, education and health care are available, and we have opportunities for enriching ourselves with spiritual, cultural, and recreational experiences.

Decency is not always easy to delineate. It can't be pinpointed with accuracy, and it varies from culture to culture. It is sometimes hard to gauge the line where decency shifts to luxury. Is a three-car family living decently, or in luxury? Four cars? Five? How about a summer house at the beach, or a winter house in Florida?

On the other side it is very clear where decency slides into the wretchedness of real poverty. That's when a person doesn't have enough to eat, or a place to sleep, can't get medical treatment, doesn't have a job, where survival is a problem every day.

The spectrum between luxury and poverty is broad. Some people in a nonviolent lifestyle decide to live toward the lower end of it and choose a poorer existence. They see it as a way of identifying more closely with those who are oppressed, who are forced to be poor. Or they want to restrict their income so they won't have to pay taxes that maintain structures of violence. Or they believe in conserving the world's resources in the interest of a more equitable distribution. They try to live simply so that others may simply live. And they find it remarkably liberating.

Others do not feel called to the lower end of the spectrum,

wanting to be relatively free from preoccupations about marginal housing, or medical insurance, or their children's education. They believe they can be more effective in altering social structures for the better if they themselves have sufficient resources to cope with life's normal challenges.

All of us need to locate ourselves somewhere in the area of decency. And we need to help others get there, too, up from the poverty in which they have been entrenched. Every person in the world should live decently. Everyone should be free from unnecessary hazards of mind and body, free to contribute to the well-being of themselves and others. One of the great challenges of personal nonviolence is to make it possible for others, as well as ourselves, to achieve this.

18

SIMPLER LIVING

If those of us trying to live more nonviolently do not choose to locate ourselves toward the poverty end of the "decency" spectrum, we still need to live more simply than middle-class American culture would have us live. If simple living is not for us, *simpler* living certainly is—simpler than the kind of living we would do if we succumbed to the temptations laid before us in the marketplace. And so we have decisions to make about our clothes, transportation, home, food, how we spend our money.

Fit for Service
In choosing to locate ourselves within the range of decency, two criteria seem especially important. The first is the need to be *fit*. If we are going to be effective, we can't afford to be bogged down, spending most of our energy on the daily demands of survival. We use our resources to meet our real needs, after we've examined those needs and cut out those that are counterfeit. We need an adequate diet and sufficient exercise. We need to be in good physical shape, and we need reliable transportation.

The second criterion is our ability to be of *service*. To build a house we have to be strong, and we have to be skilled. And so we use our resources to obtain the skills and learn the techniques to be of service. For some, this may include proficiency with a word-processor; for others it may mean taking classes in coronary-pulmonary resuscitation, or Spanish, or carpentry, or auto mechanics, or going to law school.

The two criteria merge. Our purpose in being fit should not be narcissistic, to keep the body beautiful or the spirit splendid, to feel good and be admired. Our purpose is to be *able*, so that we can better be of *service*, so that we can be part of the great nonviolent army that Gandhi envisioned, trained and skilled, ready whenever needed, "constantly engaged in constructive activities," he wrote, "ready to cope with any emergency."[1]

Jesus said, "Whoever wants to be great among you must be your servant...just as the Son of Man did not come to be served, but to serve" (Matt. 20:26,28). Our economic decisions—what kind of car to have, how much we spend on recreation, books, food, should be geared to make us *fit* for *service*.

The U.S. bishops noted this in their economics pastoral: "The fundamental moral criterion for all economic decisions...is this: They must be at the service of all people, especially the poor."[2] Their words apply not only to macro-economics—trade policies, interest rates, international loans—but also to our own personal economy, how we spend our disposable income.

A Nonviolent Diet

A steady portion of our income goes for food. Our eating pattern is a good barometer to our overall lifestyle. If we eat primarily to be fit for service, the chances are that we will do the same in other areas of life. In trying to be nonviolent, we have to watch carefully what we eat, just as we have to watch carefully what we say, how we interact with others, what we do with our time and money.

We live in a society preoccupied with food. We know that some people don't have enough, but our collective eyes are closed to the scandal of so many hungry people in the richest nation in the history of the human race. What we see instead, with the proliferation of fast food outlets and disposable containers, is what one social observer called "grazing"—people eating or drinking while they walk, drive, ride a bike, or socialize.

Many of us have a problem the opposite of Third World hunger: we are overweight. A whole new industry of commercial dieting has been spawned. After ads for bigger burgers and chicken chunks (and told how to spell relief when we eat them) have bombarded us, we are urged to try this or that miracle program to take off what the burgers and chips and chunks have put on. Then Weight Watchers comes along with what seems to be the perfect solution. One of their ads shows a trim young woman surveying a gourmet table. She says, "I can eat all this wonderful food—and still be thin." It's a miracle!

A nonviolent diet is a disciplined diet. We eat to be fit, so we avoid too much salt, too many sweets, too much fat, too many starches. We try to be nonviolent toward ourselves, so we don't make it too tough. We enjoy our food; we make sure we get enough of the right kind, and that it's pleasant to eat. We try to keep eating in its place.

Personal nonviolence involves at least some fasting. A Baptist minister friend says she always eats very little the night before she preaches. Another wonderful woman I knew in a poor Memphis neighborhood who devoted 30 years to caring for her blind and crippled husband fasted regularly one day a week.

Gandhi's fasts were legendary. Dorothy Day fasted, among other times, in Rome at the Second Vatican Council during the debate on war and peace. Cesar Chavez has fasted in support of the California farmworkers whose lives and families have been wasted by the proliferation of poisonous pesticides.

Many peace-loving people are vegetarians. They don't want to be involved in killing animals, and they don't want to be eating animals others have killed. They also find that a meatless diet is healthier, contributes to a higher energy level, is more economical, and puts them in solidarity with the majority of people in the world who can't afford to eat meat, ever. They rightly point to the misdirection of natural resources: more grain goes to fatten cattle to be slaughtered for beef in this country than is available for food in many Third and Fourth World countries. We use more fertilizer on our golf courses than all of India does on its farms.

I admire vegetarians, and always try to ask friends who come for dinner whether or not they eat meat; we prepare accordingly. We have frequent meatless meals ourselves.

But a nonviolent diet doesn't have to be meatless. Gandhi taught that sensitivity to *all* living things is a hallmark of a nonviolent person. Life extends beyond animals into the whole world of plants. So eating vegetables also involves destroying a form of life, although not as "high" a form as does eating meat or fish. A realistic assessment of the food chain includes the recognition that eating necessarily involves killing something.

The California Zen philosopher Alan Watts helped me come to terms with the destructive side of eating. He advised cultivating an attitude of respect and gratitude for those creatures whose life has been taken that I might eat. He quoted a Chinese thinker, Lin Yutang, "If a chicken has been killed, and it is not cooked properly, that chicken has died in vain." Watts went on:

> The very least I can do for a creature that has died for me is to honor it, not with an empty ritual, but by cooking it to perfection and relishing it to the full. Any animal that becomes me should enjoy itself as me....Every form of life killed for food must be husbanded and cherished. [3]

Where Our Treasure Is

Besides food, we need to take a nonviolent look at our possessions. A nonviolent person will avoid spending much time and resources on *things*: acquiring, admiring, fixing. To repair a broken faucet gives a feeling of accomplishment. And it's necessary to fix it. To assemble a model train, and build a track system for it in the basement, might well be therapeutic mechanics, necessary as a recreational diversion after a draining day.

But needed repairs and healthy hobbies are different from a preoccupation with tinkering, which can siphon off energy that would be better spent in doing something constructive for others. Jesus warned us:

> Do not store up for yourselves treasures on earth, where moth and rust destroy, and where thieves break in and steal. But store up for yourselves treasures in heaven, where moth and rust do not destroy, and where thieves do not break in and steal. For where your treasure is, there your heart will be also" (Matt. 6:19-21).

Things can easily substitute for human beings as objects of our attention and affection. It is easier to fix a machine than to mend a mind. This attitude leads us to the Strategic Defense Initiative, the Star Wars syndrome: give the nuclear threat a technological fix, rather than deal with the heart of the matter, the difficult negotiations with adversarial nations.

We are greatly tempted to acquire more property, expand and improve what we have, and spend our energy tinkering. If we want to be nonviolent, we have to make a conscious effort to resist this temptation.

Pitch In and Help

In Nicaragua and Cuba I saw first-hand the struggle to distribute land, food, education, and health care more equitably among all the people, not just those of former prestige. But financial resources in both countries are meager. Efforts are hampered by Cold War entanglements. Both countries appear poor by U.S. standards, Nicaragua *very* poor. And only a short flight away, Miami glitters, New Orleans beckons. Cubans and Nicaraguans hear from relatives who have emigrated, and they are tempted by the lure of wealth so close, seemingly so reachable. Many want to get away from their daily struggle and escape into what appears to be the promised land of shining cars and modish clothes.

A Presbyterian minister I met in Cuba said, "To be satisfied in this country today, you have to live for others." He went on to explain that to focus primarily on oneself and one's comfort, especially in a climate of consumption beamed in so many ways from the Giant to the North, is to let oneself in for constant frustration with the Cuban process. But to enter into that process in the hope that most of the Cuban people will be better off because of it gives a healthy sense of meaning and purpose, despite the inevitable hardships.

I found many wonderful people in Nicaragua, too, who had given up the comforts of Europe or North America to spend themselves to help fashion a better life for *all* the Nicaraguan people, despite the anguish of a continuing war. The treasure these people were storing up in heaven consisted in their active participation in transforming a very poor country into a more just society.

Several years ago at a conference in Europe a Swedish woman told me, "It's hard to be poor in Sweden. You really have to work at it." The social systems of her country provide housing, food, health care for everyone, whether they can afford it or not. A person who wanted to evade the social welfare system in Sweden had to make a concerted effort to do so.

I had not been to Sweden, but I had heard that its system of taxation is such that everyone with a job pays high taxes. No one is able to live at a striking level of luxury. Those who try to do so by hiding their assets in foreign bank accounts are prosecuted.

"Yes, the taxes are high," the Swedish woman said, "but I don't mind paying high taxes because I know they're going for good purposes." Like the Presbyterian minister in Cuba, she willingly supported what was good for the vast majority of her people.

For this kind of a system to work, everybody, or almost everybody, has to pitch in. When I was in Managua, the city water system was cut off twice a week. The antiquated equipment was not up to the increased demand brought on by the influx of war refugees. People were urged to be frugal with water use—toilet flushing, taking showers—and most willingly cooperated. When hundreds of thousands take part in an effort like this, it can make a difference.

We know that material possessions cannot compensate for personal insecurity, although many pursue that illusion. The vague, gnawing sense of dissatisfaction that many feel, what psychologists call "free-floating anxiety," won't be alleviated by acquiring more possessions. The quest for personal healing, if it is to have significant success, has to take us out of ourselves into constructive relationships with other people. This is what we are after when we pursue a more nonviolent lifestyle, when we strive for simpler living.

19

MONEY PROBLEMS

Theologian Paul Tillich identified two twentieth-century idols. One was nationalism, the perversion which under Hitler had driven him from his native Germany. The other was "success," that elusive state of satisfaction in pursuit of which many sacrifice friends, family, and even their own integrity.[1] Both nationalism and success are seductive goals that lure people from a healthy human life. Like the false gods of old, they command an inordinate amount of attention and reverence. Each attracts by holding out the promise that people who give allegiance to it can become better than others. If I put my nation before others—in culture, tradition, size, military might, or purity of race—then I can feel I'm among the privileged of the world.

The Idol of Success
Or if I hitch my wagon to the star of success, when I get there I know I will feel vastly superior to all those unfortunates who couldn't make it.[2]

The prime ingredient in the idol of success is money. It gives the illusion of being able to buy the other ingredients, power and prestige. The idol of success promises that one who has a great deal of money can do with it whatever one pleases, and will be admired and revered by the crowd.

This is an illusion; it doesn't work that way. Power that is bought rather than earned is prostituted power, not the kind that generates genuine allegiance. "Bought" allegience can be withdrawn and given to a higher bidder. And money can't even keep prostituted power if its possessor winds up in prison for gaining it criminally, or is suddenly stricken with an incurable disease. Jesus told us about the man who built bigger barns for his grain and his goods: "You fool! This very night your life will be demanded from you. Then who will get what you have prepared for yourself?" (Luke 12:20).

Money can evoke admiration—from those who value it highly, who respect the idol of success—but it will never buy the respect of those for whom money is not very important. In the spirit of nonviolence we know that true success does not really depend on money. Success is genuine human fulfillment, which is not an idol but the reason for our existence. The Buddhist tradition characterizes it as "enlightenment." In the Hebrew tradition success is "shalom," which is peace with God, with the world, with each other. For Christians, success is to live in harmony with God's Kingdom.

Serve God or Money

Because the Kingdom has not yet fully come and we have to live *in* this world while trying not to be thoroughly *of* it, we have to come to grips with money. Jesus said, "No one can serve two masters." We either hate the one and love the other, or are devoted to the one and despise the other. "*You cannot serve both God and Money*" (Matt. 6:24). He didn't say we can't *have* money, but he did say we can't *serve* it—and serve God at the same time. He did not say we are not to have anything to do with money, but he did say it should not dominate us so that we are preoccupied with getting or keeping it.

Because money is powerful, it is dangerous; it can grab you and take over your life. That is why it is "easier for camel to go through the eye of a needle than for a rich [person] to enter the Kingdom of God (Matt. 19:24). "But with God all things are possible" (Matt. 19:26).

How is God going to pull off this trick? Enlarge the eye of the needle? Reduce the size of the camel? No, God is going to do it by encouraging wealthy people to become less wealthy in a hurry! If you have it, use it. The nonviolent name of the game with money, as with the other accoutrements of our lifestyle, is *service*. Jesus spelled it out for a rich young man. "Go, sell everything you have and give to the poor, and you will have treasure in heaven," the treasure he talked about earlier where moth and rust do not destroy. "Then come, follow me" (Mark 10:21). Make sure your money is used to benefit others. "Give it to the poor."

I take Jesus's words not as an absolute injunction to divest of everything and become one of the wretched of the earth ourselves. That is incompatible with the rest of his teaching about the character of the Kingdom. I take his words as advice on the responsible use of one's resources, while living wherever we have located ourselves in the spectrum of decency. Jesus was speaking to a *rich* young man, who could afford to give much of of it away to help the poor.

Just as our words reveal what is in our heart, so what we do with our money is a signal of what our lives are all about, what we *are*. Where our treasure is, there our hearts are also. The responsible direction of our life is at stake in the responsible use of our money.

What to Buy

Shortly after India gained its independence from Great Britain, Gandhi advised Nehru, the new country's first Prime Minister:

> Judge every policy on how it will affect the poorest person in the poorest village. If it helps that person it's a good policy. If it doesn't help that person it's not a good policy.

Gandhi was giving a clear reference point to guide not only the laws of a nation, but the personal economies of its citizens. I go out of my way to buy Nicaraguan coffee, when I can find it; it has to be imported from the Netherlands or Canada because of the U.S. boycott of Nicaraguan products. And I prefer to fly Delta Airlines because they refused to lay off any employees during recent recessions, opting instead to take a temporary loss.

On the other side, if I know that buying a certain product contributes to exploitation in the Third World—or anywhere—I'll try not to buy it (a Wilson baseball sewn in Haiti). Or table grapes when California growers insist on using pesticides without providing precautions for the farmworkers who pick them, resulting in cancers and deformed babies.

Obviously the principle of *ahimsa* makes a nonviolent person sensitive to death-dealing organizations, and thus unwilling to contribute to their profit margin. When I learned of a particularly ugly product, like napalm which the Dow Chemical Company made during the Vietnam War, I wouldn't buy Saran Wrap, another Dow Chemical product. When I found out that Honeywell produced the cluster bombs that exploded thousands of tiny metal slivers to mutilate Vietnamese farmers, I didn't want to have anything to do with Honeywell business machines.

General Electric is heavily involved in the manufacture of nuclear weapons, so I don't like to buy GE products, such as a clock radio or their ubiquitous light bulbs. And Raytheon, the producer of friendly Amana kitchen appliances and Speed Queen washing machines, also manufactures the guidance system for the Trident nuclear submarines.

United Technologies, the parent company of Carrier air conditioners, produces the computerized command and control system for the MX missile. And I don't buy Morton's salt any more, because the Morton-Thiokol corporation, which produced the ill-fated Challenger space shuttle, also makes the propulsion systems for the missiles that deliver hydrogen bombs.

It is hard, however, to avoid cooperating with such merchants of death altogether. The second most available brand of light bulbs after GE is Sylvania, made by the GTE corporation, which also makes parts for the MX and Minuteman missiles, and does electronic warfare work for the Army[3] I don't know, either, who makes the brand of salt I buy under the label of a local supermarket chain. It still might be Morton's, with just another appearance. Or who makes the generic "light bulb, 100 watts" I can locate occasionally. And I haven't examined every other product in the weekly shopping expedition to check on its maker's social conscience. I only have so much time and I can't use it all in unearthing such facts.

So, of necessity, I am an accomplice. I buy things that contribute to the profit margin of corporations without consciences. I am uneasy about this; moral purity in all of life's details eludes me. I am trapped in much *himsa*. I have found out some things about the way the world works—and the way it should work to be congruent with the Kingdom of Heaven. I do what I can, and I know I should be doing even more, to make my lifestyle more nonviolent, to bring it more in line with the Kingdom.

PART EIGHT

NONVIOLENT IMPATIENCE

Sometimes things are so out of line with the Kingdom, so blatantly inhumane, that they get to us deeply. We burn. We are angry. And rightly so. We have to come to grips with our upsetness. We need a nonviolent way to be impatient.

20

INWARD DISCONTENT

I was taught as a child that anger is a "bad" emotion, one of the seven capital sins, along with pride, covetousness, lust and the others. So, I've often tried to ignore or suppress it. After a while, though, I began to see that anger not acknowledged is often expressed in unhealthy ways, such as a dominating drive to win in competition, or using sarcasm to make others feel inferior.

Many people say, "I can't be nonviolent, because I get angry." They—we—all need to be clear about this: anger is not the same as violence. Anger is a normal human reaction to frustration, or a spontaneous sense of indignation when something strikes us as blatantly wrong. In trying to be more nonviolent we have to be able to deal constructively with anger.

I can now accept that some of my anger is justified. There really are conditions out there that are upsetting; there really are people out there torturing others. I should feel anger about those conditions, anger at those people.

Destructive Anger

At other times, justified or not, I just *feel* angry, put out, upset. It happens when something hits me at the wrong time, in the wrong way. I had hoped for a quiet evening at home, and the phone keeps ringing. Or the neighbors are having a loud party. Or people I rely on to get a job done make a serious mistake. Some people, especially a few in public office, seem to annoy me by almost everything they do.

Getting upset is an automatic response, a reaction to frustration. I feel a surge inside; I want to lash out, somehow. My anger can be destructive. I have said things that hurt people I love. I have done physical damage, thrown things, kicked furniture. In coming to grips with this part of my shadow, I've had to face that anger, acknowledge it, grapple with it, in order not to suppress it so that it leaks out in unhealthy ways.

My anger can happen suddenly, but usually I can see it coming. I recognize the signs within myself when I feel it in my head or throat or chest. Although there may be times when a show of anger can be healthy for others who need to be sobered by seeing how hurt I am, these will be rare. Most of the time my angry outburst is going to be hurtful.

I have learned ways to keep it from exploding. One is to take a deep breath, turn away from the person or situation for a moment. If necessary, I can acknowledge straightforwardly that I'm having trouble: "I'm feeling angry and I need to take a break." Just acknowledging my anger helps to calm me down a little. If I leave the scene temporarily, and do something physical—take a dozen or so vigorous steps, go outside and walk fast—this helps release the tension within me.

If my anger springs forth uncontrolled and I say or do something unpleasant, the best remedy, when the rush is over, is to apologize. There's nothing else to do. It happened, I didn't want it to happen, I'm sorry, and I try to make amends. Later, when I have the time to reflect, I try to review the situation and see what caused it—what was the provocation, what mood was I in when it happened, what could I have done differently, how the whole things could have been handled better.

Anger to Action

But there are other times when we need to nurse our anger, keep alive the feeling of outrage when a wife is abused, unarmed protestors are clubbed, prisoners are tortured, or a child is humiliated because of color. Like the anger experienced by a young Martin Luther King. He was 14 years old when he was returning to Atlanta on a bus with his teacher after winning an oratorical contest. He described it later:

> At a small town along the way, some white passengers boarded the bus, and the white driver ordered us to get up and give the whites our seats. We didn't move quickly enough to suit him, so he began cursing us, calling us "black sons of bitches." I intended to stay right in that seat, but Mrs. Bradley finally urged me up, saying we had to obey the law. And so we stood up in the aisle for the ninety miles to Atlanta. That night will never leave my memory. It was the angriest I have ever been in my life.[1]

The young King felt anger when he was personally insulted. We can also be angry when we're not personally involved, when we see bad things happening to others. How does the following incident make you feel? According to former CIA agent John Stockwell, it really happened. American advisors in the 1970s trained Uruguayan security forces in torture techniques. They first taught the theory of torture—what kinds of electrical shocks to use, what parts of the body were most sensitive, how to inflict pain and keep the victim conscious, how far to go before the victim dies. Then they had the police go out into Montevideo late at night and pick up men and women who were wandering the streets or sleeping in parks. These helpless people were brought to the torture laboratories and used as guinea pigs to practice the techniques learned in the classroom. They were tortured until they died. Afterwards their bodies were thrown back on the streets as a warning to the citizens of Uruguay to beware of the Security Police.

When I first heard that I felt very angry. Torture is bad

enough, and as far as I'm concerned, inexcusable and unjustifiable. But here was torture to the death of the poorest of the poor—for the sake of learning how to torture better. I was angry at those who could perpetrate such cold-blooded inhumanity. I was also angry at my country whose policies in Latin America led to atrocities like this.

In Nicaragua at the end of 1987 I came to appreciate the struggling, faltering steps the government there was taking to extend literacy, housing, and medical care out into the poorest villages in the country. Consequently, I also felt angry at the constant violence that was hampering those efforts, the seemingly random attacks by the Contras on private homes, medical clinics, and farm cooperatives.

After I returned home I learned that these attacks at that particular time were the result of a deliberate policy encouraged by the U.S. State Department to concentrate on what the military calls "soft targets." The purpose of the attacks was to show Congress that the Contras were having "success" and were therefore deserving of increased funding! My anger cranked up a notch when I heard that. It made me more determined than ever to stop the violence in Nicaragua at its source, back in the United States.

Jesus got angry when he came across abuses, clearly so when he drove the money changers out of the temple. "Get these out of here! How dare you turn my Father's home into a market!" (John 2:16). He became visibly upset at some of the Pharisees also. "He looked around at them in anger...deeply distressed at their stubborn hearts" (Mark 3:5).

Paul often reacted angrily when he came across something that upset him. In Athens "he was greatly distressed to see the city full of idols" (Acts 17:16). "Greatly distressed" translates the Greek *paraxuno*, the word in the original text for Paul's feelings. It can also be translated as "stirred," "provoked," "exasperated." Paul was greatly distressed, provoked, exasperated—angry—at the idolatrous ambience of Athens, as we might be disturbed, upset—angry—today at the bullying abuses of the powerful against the powerless.

A person trying to be nonviolent can't help feeling anger—deep anger. Schillebeeckx has said that the peace of Christ, in our time, consists "in an inward discontent, in a prophetical protest against the situation as it is, and which is precisely not right the way it is."[2] It helps me to know that the anger I feel, my inward discontent when I come across appalling incidents like the Uruguayan torture training, is a form of the peace of Christ.

Anger's Energy

The person committed to nonviolence will frequently feel Schillebeeckx's "inward discontent." We feel it when we see poverty caused by economic decisions to keep land in the hands of a few to graze cattle for beef export rather than plant corn for local food. We feel it when we learn about the deliberate exploitation by dictators like the Duvaliers in Haiti who expropriated what little money the country had into their European bank accounts. We feel it when we visit Sugar Ditch in Tunica, Mississippi, and see people surviving in shaky shacks while officials debate about when to add two more lanes to the highway through the county.

We feel upset at things like this, angry at those responsible for them. In a world of warring nations, where people are tortured, and where so much injustice prevails, our reactions of anger and grief are natural and healthy. They are a form the peace of Christ increasingly takes in our day. We ought to be happy when we feel it, since it is much better than lapsing into apathy or into escapist busy-ness.

Anger is energizing. When we see something is wrong and are angry about it, we generate the energy to do something about it.[3] Anger is a powerful source for nonviolent action. Without the energy of anger we can easily become lethargic about the unrightness of our world. We can read about the troubles described in the morning paper, shrug them off: "There's nothing I can do about it." We can take "the poor you will always have with you" (Matt. 26:11) as a literal prophecy rather than a commentary on the times, and sigh with resignation. It is easy to turn away from it and stop caring, salve our consciences with many little tasks, or try to forget it all with television and our drug of choice.

Crush the Infamous Thing

If we are energized by anger we want to act. We know that the world doesn't have to be in the mess it's in. Human beings have made certain decisions—to promulgate torture, for instance—and human beings can change those decisions. Our anger impels us to work for change.

We resonate deep down to the French Revolutionaries' cry, *Ecrasez l'infame*, crush the cause of the trouble. A 73-year-old Houston man was tired of being robbed each month of his Social Security money. One night he sat up, waited for the thief, then killed him with 10 shots from his new handgun. After the shooting, he called the police. "Officer, I'll be honest, I meant to kill him." He was angry, deeply stirred by the abuse he was suffering, driven to put an end to it. We know the feeling well.

We recognize it again in the intense hostility of a crowd of Nicaraguans shortly after the fall of the Somoza regime in 1979. Several of the infamous Guardia Nacional had been captured and were being detained in the Red Cross building in Managua. An angry crowd gathered outside, and began pounding at the doors shouting for all those murderers to be brought outside so they could be lynched. Tomas Borge, the new Minister of the Interior, hurried over to the scene. As he said later, if he had wanted to please the crowd—not just those who were there, but others who had had family members brutally killed by the Guard—he would have ordered the prisoners executed. Instead, he confronted the angry shouters and demanded that they stop:

> We cannot kill these men because we carried out this revolution in order to bring an end to massacres. What's the purpose of it if we're just going to repeat what they did? In that case we would be better off never having undertaken this revolution!
>
> The crowd quieted down, and slowly, thoughtfully, disbanded.[4]

If we're trying to be nonviolent, we may sympathize with the elderly man in Houston or with the crowd who wanted to lynch the Nicaraguan guardsmen. But that's not the path we take. We recognize the trembling feeling of outrage in a righteous cause, but our challenge is to transmute that feeling into a determination to bring about constructive change. We want to make sure that our anger does not vent itself on hurting the people responsible for the atrocities. What makes us violent or nonviolent is not *feeling* anger, but what we *do* with our anger. Converting, not hurting, is our nonviolent goal.

Gandhi's nonviolence began with an experience of anger. The turning point in his life was the famous train incident in South Africa, when he was a young lawyer. He had purchased a first-class ticket for an overnight trip from Durban to Pretoria. In the middle of the night, a passenger complained about the presence of this "colored" man on the train. When Gandhi refused to go into a second-class compartment, he was unceremoniously thrown off the coach at Maritzburg, the next stop, his luggage following close behind. "That frigid night at Maritzburg," wrote one of his first biographers, "the germ of social protest was born in Gandhi."[5] It stayed with him for a lifetime.

Like Gandhi, we want to do something about abuses like this, and do it nonviolently.

21

NONVIOLENT REVENGE

We often hear people talk about "getting even." I feel like doing it myself sometimes. When I've been hurt, I want to hurt back; I want to make the smart remark that puts somebody in place, or push back when I've been pushed. It feels good to get even. "The neighbors had a loud party last weekend, so I'm going to turn up my stereo full blast this weekend. That'll show them!" Instead of "showing them," of course, all it does is irritate them—until they, in their turn, have to "get even" with me. The cycle of unpleasantness is given another push, and everybody feels a little worse. Until someone has the bright idea—and the courage—to break the cycle.

Really Getting Even

An eye for an eye and a tooth for a tooth might make sense as a restraint on revenge, its original intent in the Scriptures: only blacken an eye, don't blow off a face. But Jesus wanted the cycle of violence to be broken, so he told his followers to do something different. Instead of an eye for an eye, he said, "If someone strikes you on the right cheek, turn...the other also." If someone hits you on the right side of your face, it's going to be an insulting backhand slap, assuming the assailant is right-handed. Jesus did specify the "right" cheek. Your response, he taught, is to show them you're aware of the insult, that you won't return it, but offer them the opportunity to treat you differently by turning the other cheek (Matt 5:38-39).[1]

Break the cycle. "Do not repay anyone evil for evil" (Rom. 12:17). It takes vision and courage to react to an insult in a positive, nonviolent way.

In his Great Pacifist Paragraph, Paul gave a spiritual motive for eschewing revenge. "Do not take revenge, my friends, but leave room for God's wrath, for it is written: 'It is mine to avenge; I will repay,' says the Lord" (Rom. 12:19). If the score needs to be evened, Paul suggested, it is better to leave it to the Great Score-Evener than to take it on ourselves.

A nonviolent person will not only forego revenge, but will even go out of the way to do something nice for the one who has been hurtful. If the enemy is hungry, feed the enemy. That really takes courage. Once when Gandhi was in prison in South Africa, he made a pair of sandals and later presented them as a gift to the official responsible for putting him there, General Jan Christian Smuts. Years later General Smuts said he had been touched by the gift, that it had helped him begin to change his attitude toward Gandhi. "I have worn them for many a summer since then, even though I feel I am not worthy to stand in the shoes of so great a man."[2]

When Paul and Silas ran into trouble in Philippi, the city authorities

> ordered them to be stripped and beaten. After they had been severely flogged, they were thrown into prison, and the jailer was commanded to guard them carefully. Upon receiving such orders, he put them in the inner cell and fastened their feet in the stocks (Acts 16:22-24).

Paul undoubtedly resented such unjust treatment. Had he

made a gesture of getting even later when he had the chance, we would have understood. And he did have the chance. In the middle of the night escape suddenly became possible. So did a measure of revenge.

Suddenly there was such a violent earthquake that the foundations of the prison were shaken. At once all the prison doors flew open, and everybody's chains came loose. The jailer woke up, and when he saw the prison doors open, he drew his sword and was about to kill himself because he thought the prisoners had escaped. But Paul shouted, "Don't harm yourself! We are all here!" The jailer called for lights, rushed in and fell trembling before Paul and Silas (Acts 16:26-28).

Instead of taking advantage of the opportunity for revenge, Paul took time to console and reach out to the jailer.

Then, a few hours later, Paul made his move, because his larger purpose in Philippi was more important than settling a score with a jailer. "When it was daylight, the magistrates sent their officers to the jailer with the order: 'Release those men.' The jailer told Paul, 'The magistrates have ordered that you and Silas be released. Now you can leave. Go in peace'" (Acts 16:35-36). Instead of slipping away quietly, Paul called the city officials to task. He wanted them to see the problem they had created in treating Silas and him so abusively.

They beat us publicly without a trial, even though we are Roman citizens, and threw us into prison. And now do they want to get rid of us quietly? No! Let them come themselves and escort us out." The officers reported this to the magistrates, and when they heard that Paul and Silas were Roman citizens they were alarmed. They came to appease them and escorted them from the prison (Acts 16:35-39).

Burning Coals

Paul's "revenge" on the city officials was getting them to escort himself and Silas personally and apologetically from the very prison they had contemptuously consigned them to the day before. It was the kind of nonviolent revenge he later wrote about when he said that in giving food or drink or making some other positive gesture to an enemy, we "heap burning coals on (the enemy's) head" (Rom. 12:20).

Burning coals sounds jarringly different from what we think of as the nonviolent ideal. But they, too, can be part of the dynamics of nonviolence. Early Christian commentators, such as Jerome and Ambrose, suggested that Paul was pointing to the shame that can occur when an enemy recognizes the wrongness of the position taken, and begins to back off and to change. The shame is not our primary purpose of reaching out and helping the enemy, but it can be the first stage in their conversion process.

Heaping those burning coals is the kind of nonviolent revenge Nicaragua's Interior Minister Tomas Borge personally took shortly after the Sandinista revolution overthrew the Somoza dictatorship which had brutally tortured him, and raped and murdered his wife. He came face to face with his torturers, now prisoners themselves. As Minister of the Interior, in charge of prisons and punishment, he had the power of life and death over them. "The natural reaction," he said, "would be to gun down everyone who lived by the gun." Instead, he confronted his prisoners. "The hour of my revenge has come," he told them. "But it will be a revenge you will never forget: *we will not do you even the slightest harm!*"[3] He wanted to show them that the humanitarian ideals of the revolution were going to be put into practice immediately, despite the personal pressure he felt for revenge.

In the words of a Nicaraguan poet, "When you, practitioner of torture, can no longer so much as lift your gaze, my personal revenge will be to offer you these hands you once maltreated and without being able to make them forsake tenderness."[4] That is true nonviolent revenge, a heroic expression of the love of enemies that's at the heart of the gospel message.

◎ 22 ◎

A DIFFERENT DRUMBEAT

Daniel Berrigan has described the nonviolent approach to life as "walking to a different drumbeat." This approach is different from the crowd's.

> Its beat is complex. It commands fancy footwork....It demands that, practically, meticulously, [our nonviolent actions] be shown to connect with a grander rhythm of conscientious history—a history of sensitivity to the lives, limbs, and spiritual liberty of others.[1]

The drumbeat lets us know that people are being hurt. We want to stop the hurt—hurt to the homeless in Montevideo rounded up by the torture police, the hurt of neglect to the homeless in Memphis—so we use our political will and skill to press the U.S. government to shut down the torture schools in Uruguay, and the Memphis city administration to build shelters and provide jobs at home.

When we hear the drumbeat we feel empathy with our sisters

and brothers struggling for freedom everywhere in the world—in Uruguay and Nicaragua, in Palestine and the Philippines, in South Africa and the South Bronx. We are sensitive to those who want to leave the Soviet Union for Israel, those who would leave Vietnam for the United States, those who would leave the United States for Canada. This drumbeat reminds us of all who suffer, of perpetrators as well as victims, but it also reminds us of those who, wherever they are in the world, wherever they have been or will be in history, contribute their efforts against the tide of violence, what Berrigan called "the grander rhythm of conscientious history." We are joyful in our kinship with all who have engaged in the nonviolent struggle for freedom and justice over the centuries. "Therefore, since we are surrounded by such a great cloud of witnesses, let us throw off everything that hinders and the sin that so easily entangles, and let us run with perseverance the race marked out for us" (Heb. 12:1). We receive nourishment from this great cloud of witnesses, strength to carry on, inspiration to stay the course.

Keep On Keeping On

We will never have a perfect world, but we can certainly have a better one. Things are better for some, which is proof that they can be better for everyone. Abolition of poverty is a real possibility. A more equitable international economic system can be worked out. Dictators can be overthrown, or retired to Hawaii. Torture teams can be broken up, death squads disbanded, terrorists converted.

The nonviolent person will be impatient—angry, even—until the better world is brought about. We do not realistically expect peace and quiet, total relaxation, unruffled serenity, not until the Kingdom arrives in its fullness. There is so much to be done. Since it's important also to be nonviolent toward ourselves, we have to be realistic. Practically, most of us will focus on a single area of concern and work on it consistently, while being aware of other areas that need help as well. It could be at home or in the neighborhood: family problems or neighborhood unrest. It could be broader: civil rights, women's rights, prison reform. It could be international: Central America, the arms race. Someone with a demanding job and raising a family might find that all personal resources for the time being must be spent on immediate needs, but that person might be able to afford a financial contribution to an area of chosen involvement. The important thing is that we do *some* thing, not everything, and that we stay with it.

For Gandhi, a nonviolent struggle was worth sticking with, if those engaged in it became stronger and better for their efforts. Even taking up the struggle, he said, was a victory of sorts. A nonviolent person always wins something, he believed, even if it's only a strengthening of courage and resolve.

We do what we can. Dorothy Day saw hope in our engagement, however relatively small it might be.

> What we do is very little, but it is like the little boy with a few loaves and fishes. Christ took that little and increased it. He will do the rest. What we do is so little we may seem to be constantly failing. But so did He fail. He met with apparent failure on the Cross. But, unless the seed fall into the earth and die, there is no harvest. And why see results? Our work is to sow. Another generation will be reaping the harvest.[2]

Death and Resurrection

As we run the race marked out for us, we are painfully conscious not only of how long the course is, but also how dangerous it is. We need to face resolutely the sobering reality that running the nonviolent race, mastering the fancy footwork, and heeding the different drumbeat in a confused and jumpy world are going to create problems for us. Jesus said, "If the world hates you, keep in mind that it hated me first. If you belonged to the world, it would love you as its own. As it is, you do not belong to the world, but I have chosen you out of the world. That's why the world hates you" (John 15:18-19).

The forces who oppose us, whether anxious and uncomprehending—or callous and in cold blood—may do us in. The world's hatred can ultimately crucify us. Brazilian theologian Leonardo Boff has written:

> There are people who are too deeply attached to their quest for wealth and power that leave others out in the cold....Those with power can practice violence to defend themselves. They fashion crosses for those who fight for a world that is less divided between rich and poor. On those crosses they crucify the prophets who proclaim a greater justice, the advocates of the cause of the poor.

But whether or not they go that far, we can take comfort that our own efforts are never in vain. Everything we do, nonviolently, for someone's freedom, for justice in southern Africa or down the block, for reconciliation at home or abroad, is turning Jesus' resurrection into a living reality.

Again, Leonardo Boff:

> Wherever an authentically human life
>   is growing in the world,
> wherever justice is triumphing
>   over the instincts of domination,
> wherever grace is winning out
>   over the power of sin,
> wherever human beings are creating
>   more fraternal mediations in their life together,
> wherever love is getting the better
>   of selfish interests,
> and wherever hope is resisting
>   the lure of cynicism or despair,
> there the process of resurrection
>   is being turned into reality.
> It will continue to operate everywhere
>   until the total transfiguration of the world is achieved
>   in the definitive parousia of the Lord.[4]

What more can we ask than to be part of this grand process?

Our Cosmic Best

Years ago the French Jesuit paleontologist-philosopher Pierre Teilhard de Chardin envisioned a growing web of thought encircling the globe. He called it the "noosphere," and described it as "a harmonized collectivity of consciousness equivalent to a sort of super-consciousness. The earth," he said, "is becoming enclosed in a single thinking envelope." [5]

Of the myriad ways of thinking and acting explored in the twentieth century, the kind of active nonviolence that tries to change the world, that does change our personal world, holds the best promise of creating this "thinking envelope" envisioned by Teilhard.

It is vitally necessary to pursue this nonviolent process today. Older ways of thinking are leading to destruction—of our ecosphere, our environment, through heedless consumption of natural resources, and of our social sphere through the relentless push toward nuclear annihilation.

Pope John Paul II hit the nail on the head during his visit to Hiroshima when he said the world needs a "moral about-face....From now on it is only through a conscious choice and deliberate policy that humanity can survive."[6] Everyone needs to hear and heed the different drumbeat.

The conscious choice and deliberate policy of active nonviolence can not only save the world from nuclear catastrophe, but it can help evolve the kind of society congenial to human development. Herein lies its tremendous potential.

Nonviolence provides a challengingly satisfying attitude toward life. It doesn't urge an impossibly purist ideal of avoiding all hurt to others, but it does call us beyond being resigned to the violence in our world. It shows us another direction. Nonviolence is the *process* of peace. It is not the finished product, but it offers greater harmony in our relations with others, greater integrity within ourselves, and a sense of being part of a movement to change the world for the better.

When we undertake a knowledgeable effort to be nonviolent in all areas of life, we become part of a planetwide movement that will evolve our human history to its next, higher level.

Our personal best, in the Big Picture, turns out also to be the world's cosmic best.

NOTES

Chapter 1

1. *A Testament of Hope: The Essential Writings of Martin Luther King, Jr.* Edited by James Melvin Washington (San Francisco, Harper & Row, 1986), p. 69. Taken from King's article, "Showdown for Nonviolence," which originally appeared in *Look* magazine, Vol. 32, 16 April 1968, pp. 23-25.

2. Martin Luther King, Jr., *Strength to Love*, Ch. 5, "Loving Your Enemies" (New York: Simon and Schuster, Pocket Books Memorial Edition, 1964), pp. 42-43.

3. *Habits of the Heart: Individualism and Commitment in American Life*, by Robert N. Bellah, R. Madsen, W.M. Sullivan, A. Swidler, and S.M. Tipton (New York: Harper & Row, Perennial Library Edition, 1985), pp. 286-290.

Chapter 2

1. *A Testament of Hope: The Essential Writings of Martin Luther King, Jr.* Edited by James Melvin Washington (San Francisco: Harper & Row, 1986), p. 19. Taken from King's article, "An Experiment in Love," which originally appeared in *Jubilee*, September, 1958, pp. 11 ff.

2. Dogmatic Constitution on the Church (*Lumen Gentium*), para. #9.

3. Alfred Bloom, "Spiritual Potentials for Quality Living," in *The Pacific World*: Journal of the Institute of Buddhist Studies, Fall, 1986, p. 43.

4. Mohandas K. Gandhi, *Non-violent Resistance* (New York: Schocken Books, 1961), p. 133.

5. Gail Buchalter, "Why I Bought a Gun," in the Sunday *Parade* magazine, February 21, 1988, p. 5.

Chapter 3

1. Thomas Merton, *Conjectures of a Guilty Bystander* (New York: Doubleday, 1966) p. 72.

2. Gandhi's meaning of truth is discussed in *Fighting with Gandhi*, by Mark Juergensmeyer (San Francisco: Harper & Row, 1984), Chapter 3, pp. 18-26.

Notes

3. Pastoral Constitution on the Church in the Modern World (*Gaudium et Spes*), para. #55.

4. Mohandas K. Gandhi, *An Autobiography* (Boston: Beacon Press, 1957), p. 349.

5. Quoted by Martin Luther King, Jr., *A Testament of Hope: The Essential Writings of Martin Luther King, Jr.* Edited by James Melvin Washington (San Francisco: Harper & Row, 1986), p. 18. Taken from King's article, "An Experiment in Love," which originally appeared in *Jubilee*, September, 1958, pp. 11 ff.

Chapter 4

1. *A Testament of Hope: The Essential Writings of Martin Luther King, Jr.* Edited by James Melvin Washington (San Francisco: Harper & Row, 1986), p. 349. This section originally appeared as a "Playboy Interview: Martin Luther King," in *Playboy*, January 1965, pp. 117 ff.

2. Jim Douglass, "Wither the White Train?" in *Ground Zero*, Vol. 6, No. 4, Winter 1988, p. 8.

Chapter 5

1. Edward Schillebeeckx, O.P., "Revelation in Word and Deed," in *The Word: Readings in Theology* (New York: P.J. Kenedy and Sons, 1964), p. 258.

Chapter 6

1. These patterns are discussed in "The Perfect Conversation" and "Control of Conversation" in *More on the Gentle Art of Verbal Self-Defense*, by Suzette Haden Elgin (Englewood Cliffs, N.J.: Prentice-Hall, 1983), pp. 13-19.

Chapter 7

1. An expanded discussion of this defensive reaction, is given in *Criticizing*, by William J. Diehm (Minneapolis: Augsburg Publishing House, 1986), especially p. 62.

2. Martin Luther King, Jr., *Why We Can't Wait* (New York: Mentor Books, 1964 edition), p. 79.

3. "Truth, Power of Peace," Message of His Holiness Pope John Paul II for the celebration of the Day of Peace, January 1980, para. #3.

Chapter 8

1. Joan Turner Beifuss, *At the River I Stand: Memphis, the 1968 Strike, and*

Martin Luther King. (Memphis: B & W Books, 1985), p. 254.

2. *A Testament of Hope: The Essential Writings of Martin Luther King, Jr.* Edited by James Melvin Washington (San Francisco: Harper & Row, 1986), p. 372.

Chapter 9

1. Thich Nhat Hanh, "Being Peace: Thoughts for Peace Workers and Others," in *Fellowship*, July/August, 1986, p. 6.

2. Bernice S. Siegel, M.D., *Love, Medicine and Miracles* (New York: Harper & Row, 1986), p. 3.

Chapter 10

1. For a broader discussion on the differences between assertion and aggression, see *Your Perfect Right: A Guide to Assertive Living*, Robert E. Alberti and Michael L. Emmons (San Luis Obispo, Ca.: Impact Publishers, 1986 edition). Especially chapters 4 and 5.

Chapter 11

1. Edward Schillebeeckx, O.P., "Revelation in Word and Deed," in *The Word: Readings in Theology* (New York: P.J. Kenedy and Sons, 1964), p. 270.

2. This story is told in *Rape Avoidance and Resistance, A Nonviolent Approach*, by Mary Crane (San Francisco: Peace and Gladness Press, 1982), p. 44.

3. *A Testament of Hope: The Essential Writings of Martin Luther King, Jr.* Edited by James Melvin Washington (San Francisco: Harper & Row, 1986), p. 10. Taken from King's article, "An Experiment in Love," which first appeared in *Jubilee*, September, 1958, p. 11 ff.

4. The concept of trust is analyzed in Leroy H. Pelton, *The Psychology of Nonviolence* (New York: Pergamon Press, 1974), p. 205.

Chapter 12

1. This story is told in *Reweaving the Web of Life: Feminism and Nonviolence*, edited by Pam McAllister (Philadelphia: New Society Publishers, 1982), p. 382.

Chapter 13

1. For a summary of Maggie Pharris's story see her letter in *Way of Peace:*

A Guide to Nonviolence, edited by Gerard A. Vanderhaar and Mary Lou Kownacki, OSB (Erie, PA., Pax Christi USA, 1987), p. 72.

2. Richard B. Gregg, *The Power of Nonviolence* (London: James Clarke and Co., Second Revised Edition, 1960), p. 44.

Chapter 14

1. For more information on Pax Christi's Video and Training Workshops on Nonviolent Responses to Personal Assault, contact Pax Christi USA, 348 E. 10th St., Erie, Pa. 16503, tel. (814) 453-4955.

Chapter 15

1. Harvey Cox, *The Secular City* (New York: MacMillan, paperback edition, 1965), p. 45.

2. "Resolve to be a Civil Creature," by Ellen Goodman, in *The Commercial Appeal*, Memphis, Jan. 6, 1987, p. A-8.

3. A helpful discussion of body language is given in chapter 8 of *More on the Gentle Art of Verbal Self-Defense*, by Suzette Haden Elgin (Englewood Cliffs, N.J., Pretice-Hall, 1983).

4. See Arch Lustberg, *Winning at Confrontation* (Washington, D.C., U.S. Chamber of Commerce, 1984), p. 31.

Chapter 16

1. Louis Fischer, *The Life of Mahatma Gandhi* (New York: MacMillian, Collier Books edition, 1962), p. 277.

2. For more of the same, see "Humor for Peace," by Gary Zimmerman, in *Working for Peace: A Handbook of Practical Psychology and Other Working Tools*, edited by Neil Wollman (San Luis Obispo, Ca.: Impact Publishers, 1985), pp. 246-251.

3. Avner Ziv, *Personality and Sense of Humor* (New York: Springer Publishing Co., 1984), p. 62.

Chapter 17

1. Encyclical Letter, *Sollicitudo Rei Socialis*, 30 December 1987, para. #10.

Chapter 18

1. Mohandas K. Gandhi, *Non-Violent Resistance* (New York: Schocken Books, 1961), p. 86.

2. "Economic Justice for All," the U.S. Bishop's Pastoral Letter on Catholic Social Teaching and the U.S. Economy, November 14, 1986, para #24.
3. Alan Watts, *Does It Matter?* (New York: Random House, Vintage Books edition, 1971), p. 28.

Chapter 19

1. Paul Tillich, *The Dynamics of Faith* (New York: Harper & Row, Torchbook edition, 1957), pp. 1, 3.
2. See the critique of this kind of "success" in *The Healing Power of Nonviolence*, by Bernard Haring (New York: Paulist Press, 1986), p. 76.
3. See *Rating America's Corporate Conscience*, by Steven D. Lydenberg et al. (Reading, Mass.: Addison-Wesley Publishing Co., 1986), pp. 416-417.

Chapter 20

1. *A Testament of Hope: The Essential Writings of Martin Luther King, Jr.* Edited by James Melvin Washington (San Francisco: Harper & Row, 1986), p. 343. This section originally appeared as a "Playboy Interview: Martin Luther King," in *Playboy*, January, 1965, pp. 117 ff.
2. Edward Schillebeeckx, O.P., "In Seearch of the Salvific Value of a Political Praxis of Peace," in *Peace Spirituality for Peacemakers* (Antwerp, Belgium: Omega Press, 1985), p. 25.
3. Cf. Harriet Goldhor Lerner, *The Dance of Anger* (New York: Harper & Row, 1985), p. 189.
4. *Christianity and Revolution: Thomas Borge's Theology of Life*, edited and translated by Andrew Reding (Maryknoll, N.Y.: Orbis Books, 1987), p. 26.
5. Louis Fischer, *The Life of Mahatma Gandhi* (New York: MacMillan, Collier Books edition, 1962), p. 49.

Chapter 21

1. For this explanation of Jesus' advice to turn the other cheek, I am indebted to Walter Wink. See his *Violence and Nonviolence in South Africa: Jesus' Third Way* (Philadelphia: New Society Publishers, 1987), Chapter Two, especially p. 15.
2. Louis Fischer, *The Life of Mahatma Gandhi* (New York: MacMillan, Collier Books edition, 1962), p. 125.
3. *Christianity and Revolution: Tomas Borge's Theology of Life*, edited and translated by Andrew Reding (Maryknoll, N.Y.: Orbis Books, 1987), p. 24.

4. Luis Enrique Mejia Godoy, "My Personal Revenge." Quoted at the beginning of *Christianity and Revolution: Tomas Borge's Theology of Life.*

Chapter 22

1. Daniel Berrigan, *Ten Commandments for the Long Haul* (Nashville: Abingdon, 1981), p. 100.
2. Quoted by Carl Siciliano, "The Little Way of St. Therese of Lisieux," *The Catholic Worker*, March, 1987, p. 7.
3. Leonardo Boff, *Way of the Cross—Way of Justice* (Maryknoll, N.Y.: Orbis Books, 1982), p. 16.
4. *Ibid.*, p. 126.
5. Pierre Teilhard de Chardin, *The Phenomenon of Man* (New York, Harper & Row, Torchbook edition, 1961), p. 251.
6. "Address to Scientists and Scholars," quoted in *The Challenge of Peace: God's Promise and Our Response*, the U.S. Catholic Bishop's Pastoral Letter on War and Peace, May 3, 1983, para. #3.

BIBLIOGRAPHY

Abbott, Walter M. *The Documents of Vatican II*. New York: The America Press, 1966.

Alberti, Robert E., and Emmons, Michael L. *Your Perfect Right: A Guide to Assertive Living*. San Luis Obispo, Cal: Impact Publishers, 1986.

Barnaby, Frank, ed. *The Gaia Peace Atlas: Survival into the Third Millenium*. New York: Doubleday, 1988.

Beifuss, Joan Turner. *At the River I Stand: Memphis, the 1968 Strike, and Martin Luther King*. Memphis: B & W Books, 1985.

Bellah, Robert, et al. *Habits of the Heart: Individualism and Commitment in American Life*. New York: Harper & Row, 1985.

Berrigan Daniel. *Ten Commandments for the Long Haul*. Nashville: Abingdon, 1981.

_____. *The Words Our Savior Gave Us*. Springfield, Ill.: Templegate, 1978.

Bickmore, Kathy, et al. *Alternatives to Violence: A Manual for Teaching Peacemaking to Youths and Adults*. Cleveland: Cleveland Friends Meeting, 1984.

Boff, Leonardo. *Way of the Cross—Way of Justice*. Maryknoll, N.Y.: Orbis Books, 1982.

Burton, John W. *Resolving Deep-Rooted Conflice: A Handbook*. Lanham, Md.: University Press of America, 1987.

Cooney, Robert, and Michalowski, Helen. *Power of the People: Active Nonviolence in the United States*. Culver City, Cal.: Peace Press, Inc., 1977.

Cox, Harvey. *The Secular City*. New York: Macmillan, 1965.

Day, Dorothy. *The Long Loneliness*. Garden City, N.Y.: Image Books, 1959.

Diehm, William J. *Criticizing*. Minneapolis: Augsburg, 1986.

Elgin, Suzette Haden. *More on the Gentle Art of Verbal Self-Defense*. Englewood Cliffs, N.J.: Prentice Hall, 1983.

Fahey, Joseph, and Armstrong, Richard. *A Peace Reader: Essential Readings on War, Justice, Non-Violence and World Order*. Mahwah, N.J.: Paulist Press, 1987.

Ferguson, John. *War and Peace in the World's Religions*. New York: Oxford University Press, 1978.

Fischer, Louis. *The Life of Mahatma Gandhi*. New York: Macmillan, 1962 (first published in 1950).

Fisher, Roger, and Ury, William. *Getting to Yes: Negotiating Agreement Without Giving In*. New York: Penguin Books, 1983.

Gandhi, Mohandas K. *An Autobiography*. Boston: Beacon Press, 1957.

_____. *Non-Violent Resistance*. New York: Schocken Books, 1961.

Gregg, Richard B. *The Power of Nonviolence*. London: James Clarke and Co., 1960.

Häring, Bernard. *The Healing Power of Nonviolence*. Mahway, N.J.: Paulist Press, 1986.

Jurgensmeyer, Mark. *Fighting With Gandhi: A Step-by-Step Strategy for Resolving Everyday Conflicts*. San Francisco: Harper & Row, 1984.

Kahn, Sandra Lynn. *Peacemaking: A Systems Approach to Conflict Management*. Lanham, Md: University Press of America, 1988.

King, Martin Luther, Jr. *Strength to Love*. New York: Pocket Books, 1986.

_____. *Why We Can't Wait*. New York: New American Library, 1964.

Küng, Hans. *On Being a Christian*. New York: Doubleday, 1976.

Lerner, Marriet Goldhor. *The Dance of Anger*. New York: Harper & Row, 1985.

Lustbert, Arch. *Winning at Confrontation*. Washington, D.C.: U.S. Chamber of Commerce, 1984.

Lydenberg, Steven D., et al. *Rating America's Corporate Conscience*. Reading, Mass.: Addison-Wesley, 1986.

Merton, Thomas. *Conjectures of a Guilty Bystander*. New York: Doubleday, 1966.

_____. *Faith and Violence*. Notre Dame, Ind.: University of Notre Dame Press, 1968.

McAllister, Pam, ed. *Reweaving the Web of Life: Feminism and Nonviolence*. Philadelphia: New Society Publishers, 1982.

Pelton, Leroy H. *The Psychology of Nonviolence*. New York: Pergamon Press, 1974.

Piaget, Gerald W., and Binkley, Barbara. *How to Communicate Un-*

der Pressure: Dealing Effectively with Difficult People. Portola Valley, Cal.: IAHB Press, 1982.

Reding, Andrew, ed. *Christianity and Revolution: Thomas Borge's Theology of Life.* Maryknoll, N.Y.: Orbis Books, 1987.

Schillebeeckx, Edward. *Ministry: Leadership in the Community of Jesus Christ.* New York: Crossroad, 1981.

Siegel, Bernie S. *Love, Medicine and Miracles.* New York: Harper & Row, 1986.

Teilhard de Chardin, Pierre. *Building the Earth.* Wilkes-Barre, Penn.: Dimension Books, 1965.

_____. *The Phenomenon of Man.* New York: Harper & Row, 1959.

Tillich, Paul. *The Dynamics of Faith.* New York: Harper & Row, 1957.

Vanderhaar, Gerard A. *Christians and Nonviolence in the Nuclear Age.* Mystic, Conn.: Twenty-Third Publications, 1982.

_____, and Kownacki, Mary Lou, eds. *Way of Peace: A Guide to Nonviolence.* Erie, Penn.: Pax Christi USA, 1987.

Washington, James M., ed. *A Testament of Hope: The Essential Writings of Martin Luther King, Jr..* San Francisco, Harper & Row, 1986.

Watts, Alan. *Does It Matter?* New York: Random House, 1971.

Wink, Walter. *Violence and Nonviolence in South Africa: Jesus' Third Way.* Philadelphia: New Society Publishers, 1987.

Wollman, Neil. *Working for Peace: A Handbook of Practical Psychol-

ogy and Other Tools. San Luis Obispo, Cal.: Impact Publishers, 1985.

Yoder, John H., et al. *What Would You Do? If a Violent Person Threatened to Harm a Loved One.* Scottdale, Penn.: Herald Press, 1983.

Ziv, Avner. *Personality and Sense of Humor.* New York: Springer Publisher Co., 1984.

Shorter Works

Bloom, Alfred. "Spiritual Potentials for Quality Living," in *The Pacific World: Journal for the Institute of Buddhist Studies.* Fall, 1986.

Buchalter, Gail. "Why I Bought a Gun," in the Sunday *Parade* magazine, February 21, 1988.

Crane, Mary. *Rape Avoidance and Resistance: A Nonviolent Approach.* Pamphlet, published by the Peace and Gladness Press, San Francisco, 1982.

Douglass, Jim. "Wither the White Train?" in *Ground Zero,* Vol. 6, No. 4, Winter 1988.

Goodman, Ellen. "Resolve to Be a Civil Creature," in *The Commercial Appeal,* Memphis, January 6, 1987.

Hanh, Thich Nhat. "Being Peace: Thoughts for Peace Workers and Others," in *Fellowship,* July/August 1986.

John Paul II. "Truth, Power of Peace," Message for the 1980 World Day of Peace.

_____. Encyclical Letter *Sollicitudo Rei Socialis,* [On Social Concern] 30 December 1987.

Schillebeeckx, Edward. "Revelation in Word and Deed, " in *The Word: Readings in Theology*. New York. P.J. Kenedy and Sons, 1964.

_____. "In Search of the Salvific Value of a Political Praxis of Peace," in *Peace Spirituality for Peacemakers*. Antwerp, Belgium: Omega Press, 1985.

U.S. Catholic Bishops. *The Challenge of Peace: God's Promise and Our Response*, Pastoral Letter on War and Peace, May 3, 1983.

_____. *Economic Justice for All*, Pastoral Letter on Catholic Social Teaching and the U.S. Economy, November 14, 1986.

Vanderhaar, Gerard A. *Nonviolence: Theory and Practice*. Pamphlet published by the Mid-South Peace and Justice Center, Memphis, 1985.

Critical Acclaim for Gerard Vanderhaar's *Christians and Nonviolence in the Nuclear Age* (Twenty-Third Publications):

"Gerard Vanderhaar presents a clear...argument for this [nonviolent] solution to the arms race."

William H. Millerd
America

"If you're instinctively against the madness of the nuclear arms race, but don't have the background to feel competent discussing why, this...will get you started in the right direction."

Anne Bingham
National Catholic News Service

"This substantive paperback deserves peacemakers' attention."

Howard W. Lull
The Churchman

"...a timely resource....Both adults and teens will find the contents useful. The discussion questions for each chapter are thought-provoking and will raise consciousness to the issues and motivate individuals to work for peace."

Sister M. Frye, MHSH
Dimensions of Ministry

"While this study does present a theoretical framework for Christian thinking in regard to war...its greater contribution may be its *practicality*....The examples are concrete and realistic and spiritually sound."

James J. Higgins, C.SS.R.
Liguorian

What Reviewers have said about Gerard Vanderhaar's *Enemies and How to Love Them* (Twenty-Third Publications):

"...a book well worth reading. It doesn't take long. And it offers a wealth of insight into the meaning Jesus' words have for us today."
Roger S. Powers
Fellowship

"The language is easy to read and generally non-theological. Study questions are included, making it a useful tool for study groups on peace issues, reconciliation, and forgiveness."
Maryanne A. Hanak
Emmanuel

"...makes for good reading and sharing."
Sr. Clara Fehringer, O.S.U.
Sisters Today

"Vanderhaar is among the avante-garde....The book is well organized, clearly written, and engaging."
J. Milburn Thompson
Horizons

"...an excellent book....There are numerous encouraging examples, insights, and practical suggestions to benefit everyone."
Michael Friend
The Advocate

"...'must reading' to counteract *Reader's Digest* mentality, William Buckley's arrogance, and the *New York Times's* putative 'realism.'"
Warren E. Steinkraus
Journal of Social Philosophy